A
Voluptuous
God

Robert V. Thompson

A Voluptuous God

A Christian Heretic Speaks

CopperHouse

Editor: Ingrid Turnbull
Cover and interior design: Verena Velten
Cover artwork: *Hope in the Desert: 2* by Jennifer Andrews.
   Copyright © 1998 Jennifer Andrews. jandrews@gil.com.au,
   www.brizart.com.au. Used by permission.
Pre-press production: Chaunda Daigneault
Proofreader: Dianne Greenslade

CopperHouse is an imprint of Wood Lake Publishing, Inc.
Wood Lake Publishing acknowledges the financial support
of the Government of Canada, through the Book Publishing
Industry Development Program (BPIDP) for its publishing
activities. Wood Lake Publishing also acknowledges the
financial support of the Province of British Columbia through the
Book Publishing Tax Credit.

BNC CERTIFIED | BIBLIOGRAPHIC DATA 2007-08

At Wood Lake Publishing, we practise what we publish, being
guided by a concern for fairness, justice, and equal opportunity
in all of our relationships with employees and customers. Wood
Lake Publishing is an employee-owned company, committed
to caring for the environment and all creation. Wood Lake
Publishing recycles, reuses, and encourages readers to do the
same. Resources are printed on 100% post-consumer recycled
paper and more environmentally friendly groundwood papers
(newsprint), whenever possible.
A percentage of all profit is donated to charitable organizations.

Library and Archives Canada Cataloguing in Publication

Thompson, Robert V., 1948-
A voluptuous God : a Christian heretic speaks /
Robert V. Thompson.
Includes bibliographical references.
ISBN 978-1-55145-558-7
1. Spirituality. 2. Spiritual life – Christianity. 3. Christian life.
4. Self-actualization (Psychology) – Religious aspects. I. Title.
BV4501.3.T563 2007   248   C2007-903911-1

Published by CopperHouse
An imprint of Wood Lake Publishing Inc.
9590 Jim Bailey Road, Kelowna, BC, Canada, V4V 1R2
www.woodlakebooks.com
250.766.2778

Printing 10 9 8 7 6 5 4 3 2 1
Printed in Canada by Houghton Boston

Permissions

Quotations from the Bible are taken
from the New Revised Standard Version
of the Bible, copyright 1989 by the
Division of Christian Education of the
National Council of Churches of Christ
in the USA, all rights reserved, used by
permission.

The poem *I thank You God for most this
amazing* by e. e. cummings Copyright
© 1950, 1978, 1991 by the Trustees for
the e. e. cummings Trust. Copyright ©
1979 by George James Firmage, from
Complete Poems: 1904–1962 by e. e.
cummings, edited by George J. Firmage.
Used by permission of Liveright
Publishing Corporation.

Excerpt from *Manifesto: The Mad Farmer
Liberation Front* from *Collected Poems
1957–1982* by Wendell Berry. Copyright
© 1985 by Wendell Berry. Reprinted
by permission of North Point Press, a
division of Farrar, Straus and Giroux,
LLC.

In Memoriam
Brother Wayne Teasdale
Interspiritual Wayne energy lives in, among, and through us

To the Lake Street Church of Evanston
You are the book I keep reading

Gratitudes

••• ❧❧❧ •••

Meister Eckhart once said, "If the only prayer you ever say in your entire life is thank you, it will be enough."

I'm very happy that Meister Eckhart said that, because, as time rolls on, "thank you" is the only prayer that makes sense to me.

It has been a delight to work with the Wood Lake Publishing team. Their ability to hear my voice and understand my message, to ask the right questions, and to remain open to my own questions and responses, has been such a great gift. I am particularly grateful to my editor, Ingrid Turnbull. I'll never forget one round of e-mail exchanges in which Ingrid offered some truly significant insights. I complimented her and asked, "Who shall I tell that you deserve a raise?" Her one-word response was, "God."

A shared sense of humour makes light the load and joyous the journey. Thank you, dear Wood Lake friends.

Well over a decade ago a number of members of my congregation told me that I should write a book. I thought they were joking but I thanked them and wondered what I could possibly say that would fill a book. Nevertheless, they got my attention.

Over the years this congregation has questioned my answers, challenged my assumptions and supported most of my conclusions. I am allegedly their spiritual teacher. But it is actually the other way around. This vibrant group has taught me that life is inescapably spiritual. They have taught me how to find meaning when life seems meaningless. They have taught me that there is an innate and irrevocable Divine presence available to all of us in every experience, if only we are open to it. This spiritual community known as the Lake Street Church of Evanston makes my heart sing.

I would be remiss not to mention the incredible Lake Street Church staff. These friends and colleagues have gone out of their way to cover for me so I could write this book. Without their support I couldn't have done it. How does one sufficiently say "thank you" for that kind of fidelity?

All of my circles of gratitude are connected. A profound thank you to my friend Mirabai Starr, who has bestowed on me many gifts, not the least of which have been her unflagging support and encouragement throughout this process. To Carlyle Carter for helping me to form the original book proposal, to Mary Alice Ball for being my fact-checker extraordinaire, and to Hema Pokharna for being so wonderfully supportive of this project – thank you!

Our children – Sarah Thompson and her husband, Satoshi Matsushita; Leah Thompson and her partner, Jeremy James; Jason Carter and his wife, Kate; and Sarah Carter and her husband, Brendan Murphy – have each in their own way supported me throughout the evolution of this project. And our grandsons, Kai Matsushita and Henry Carter, show us through their young and effervescent lives that they are the greatest heretics of all. Living fully out of their own experience, they remind me to laugh, love, and give thanks for life.

My sister Jan Thompson Moses and her husband, Jay Moses, became involved early on in the book-writing process, reading and critiquing early versions of my manuscript. Their clarity and honesty helped me immeasurably, and to them I am indebted.

Finally, I offer the prayer "thank you" to and for my spouse and life partner, Judy Langford. At once, Judy consoles me and calls me to stretch. She confirms who I am while inviting me to see that I am more than I can ever imagine. More than anyone, Judy has taught me to trust the heart, to live through the heart, to think through the heart. The heart is a heretic and Judy is my heart's original and continuing teacher.

For all of this and more, I have only one prayer: "Thank you."

Contents

Introduction

My father, who is a World War II veteran, often tells us stories about the war. We've heard many of them so many times that we could provide the punchlines. Recently, however, he surprised us with a new story. He told us about a time when he and his buddy were lying in a foxhole and began taking fire. They were both pinned to the ground by incoming bullets whizzing overhead. My father looked over and saw his buddy lying there, shaking uncontrollably.

"Hey, Joe!" my father shouted, "Are you all right?"

Teeth chattering, Joe yelled back, "I'm scared to death."

A few days later, my father and Joe were walking through a shoulder-high trench. Their assignment was to look for enemy soldiers in the trench and take them captive if possible. If capturing them alive was not possible, they were to kill them. Joe and my father walked gingerly through the trench, rifles pointing ahead, ready to fire.

They soon spotted a lone German soldier crouched in a crevice in the mud. He was trembling so violently he could scarcely hold himself together. Joe and my father motioned to him to stand up. When the soldier realized they weren't going to shoot him, his countenance immediately changed. He stopped shaking. The German soldier went through a transfiguration.

During the telling of this story, my Dad's eyes got bigger, his mannerisms became more animated, and the tone of his voice altered. "It was amazing. I can see the change in that soldier's countenance to this very day," he said.

We all sat silently in the living room for a little while before I asked, "Dad, what did you experience when you looked into that soldier's eyes?"

My father was surprised by the question. He paused and thought a moment. Then he looked up and said, "Compassion. Yes, I felt enormous compassion for that German soldier."

A Voluptuous God: A Christian Heretic Speaks reaches out to the place from where the heart is beckoning as we search for universal truth. It wrestles with what it means to be a spiritual being on a human journey. It offers questions and asks the reader to respond by exploring the innermost recesses of the heart, where we belong to God and each other. It is while wrestling with the questions that God is revealed as the mystery that defines and redefines life.

A Voluptuous God shares the message that spiritual truth is something we discover within ourselves as we experience life. It is our connection to life.

This book celebrates the rich Christian tradition of free thinkers and seekers whose voices have often been stifled by those in positions of authority, or muffled by the dominant religious ethos of the culture.

A member of my congregation, who has had several harrowing life experiences, likes to say that religion is for those who want to go to heaven, whereas spirituality is for those who have been to hell. I think she is distinguishing between religion of the head and religion of the heart.

Religion of the head involves thinking about life's questions in order to come up with answers. Religion of the heart is about seeing our innate and unalterable connection to all others as both the question and the answer. The heart is a compass that points to specific experiences that carry universal meaning, beyond doctrinal formula.

Heretics are people who deviate from the norm. The word heretic comes from the Greek word *haireses*, meaning "to choose." Heretics choose a path that differs from the norm. Jesus was a Jewish heretic, and Christianity began as a Jewish heresy.

There is a story in the gospels of some teachers of orthodoxy who confronted Jesus, saying, "We understand your disciples are picking grain and that you are healing people on the Sabbath, our holy day of rest. Don't you know that's against the beliefs and rules of our religion?"

Jesus replied, "People were not made to serve the Sabbath; the Sabbath was made to serve people."[1]

This was heresy.

To be a soldier and to feel compassion for the enemy in time of war is an example of what a heretic does. Soldiers are trained in military dogma, but the heart cannot be trained, only opened.

My father received a flash of spiritual insight in that trench in Germany. No one could tell him what to believe, what to feel, what to think. The feeling of compassion just overwhelmed him. When he saw that trembling enemy soldier, no verse of scripture came to him, no Christian doctrine filled his head. He found himself caught up in a moment that transcended religion, culture, and political ideology. The heart took over and became the arbiter of his experience. He was living through his heart during that moment in the trenches.

Religious orthodoxy is the inevitable result of thinking exclusively from the head. The heart is always a heretic, however, and its natural inclination is to upend the status quo. The heart sees the human race as one, regardless of belief, doctrine, religion, class, or sexual orientation. Distinctions of "us-versus-them" dissolve when we see each other through the heart. Heretics know that the mystery of life cannot be shrink-wrapped, the beauty of life cannot be limited to canvas, and that the quest for meaning requires taking risks and making sacrifices. This is why heretics refuse to allow those in authority to speak for them.

The heart is a heretic because it seeks unity of spirit, not uniformity of thinking. To listen to the heart is an act of conscience; to open to it is an act of courage. To take whole-hearted action in our daily lives means we have the power to transform not only ourselves but also the world we live in. Inevitably, heretics are people who think through the heart.

While rooted in the Christian tradition, *A Voluptuous God* affirms that truth is found in other religious and spiritual traditions, as well as in the secular expressions of human experience. This is why I have included references and stories from a variety of religious and spiritual traditions. There is one truth and its manifestations are multiple.

I invite you to join me on this journey of discovery. I hope this book will open you to your questions. And I hope that your questions will spring out from your own experiences, and lead you to new and deeper places of connection.

In this regard, I believe the poet Ranier Maria Rilke is right.[2] When we love the questions, in some inexplicable way we live ourselves into answers we never could have imagined.

[1] (Mark 2:27)
[2] Ranier Maria Rilke, *Letters to a Young Poet*, M. D. Herter Norton, translator (WW Norton, 2004)

PART I

God: The Answer Is the Question

... ❦ ...

I believe the power of God is lodged in the very marrow of our substance and is pressing, constantly pressing, for release in order to permeate every fiber of our being.

~ WILLIAM SLOANE COFFIN, *CREDO* (WESTMINSTER JOHN KNOX PRESS, 2004)

*Awareness of God does not come by degrees
from timidity to intellectual temerity;
it is not a decision reached at the crossroads of doubt.
It comes when, drifting in the wilderness,
having gone astray,
we suddenly behold the immutable polar star.
Out of endless anxiety,
out of denial and despair.
The soul bursts out in speechless crying.*

~ RABBI ABRAHAM JOSHUA HESCHEL, *I ASKED FOR WONDER* (CROSSROAD, 1991)

1

For a Good Time, Call God

$$\cdots \; \text{❧❀❧} \; \cdots$$

Sometimes I think I must be wearing a scarlet "H" around my neck. "H" for heretic. I say this because it seems that I am often asked the kind of questions that most of my ministerial colleagues seldom receive. For example, a member of my congregation recently wanted to know if I believed in God. I was surprised to be asked this question since I am a minister, but it reminded me that God is a loaded word. This is why I always answer that question by saying that it depends on what is meant by God.

If I'm being asked about whether or not I believe in some supreme being with an extreme ego who insists that people conform to a rigid dogma, I say, "No, I don't believe in that God."

If I'm asked if I believe in a God whose abode is in a heaven, separated from the earthly domain, the answer is, "No, I don't believe in that God."

If the question is if I believe in a God who uses coercive power to make things happen a certain way, I reply, "Not that one either."

Most people who say they believe in God agree that God is spirit, but the word spirit is utterly abstract. This is why we resort to metaphors.

In conventional Christianity, the prevailing metaphor for God is "Our Father who art in heaven." Here is a metaphor that says God is distant from, or better yet, above us. After all, heaven is a far-off place, and that's where God is. The heavenly father of this metaphor is removed from human experience and insists that "it's my way or the highway."

I know that God as heavenly father is meaningful to many. But it's all too easy to get an image fixed in our minds and to believe it's true because we have been conditioned to believe it or because it suits us.

This reminds me of the story of a woman who reportedly had a mystical experience and told a friend, "I saw God last night."

"Really?" her friend asked. "What's he like?"

"Well," she answered, "he's a woman and she's black!"

This little ditty that circulated in the 1980s is in itself indicative of the power of metaphor. We laughed because we were surprised by the punchline. Thoroughly conditioned by the metaphor of a father in heaven, we had also assumed that a father in heaven was a white guy in the sky.

In classical terms, mysticism is the direct intuition or experience of God or ultimate reality. A mystic's beliefs are centred not on any rational religious doctrine but on the direct experience of unity with ultimate reality. In the 14th century, the Rhineland mystic Meister Eckhart coined a metaphor for God that was as scandalous then as it is now. Meister Eckhart said, "God is voluptuous and delicious."[1]

Meister Eckhart used this metaphor not to be shocking or heretical. He was simply saying that, in his experience, God is voluptuous. In his experience, God is delicious. In his experience, to be near to God is to have a good time. He knew that God takes pleasure in simple things.

God delights in little things. God knows that laughter is the best medicine, that love heals us and that joy causes our hearts to take flight. The metaphor of a voluptuous Divine calls us to laughter, love, and joy.

Here's to a God who giggles with delight, who tickles creation in order to waken it to the pleasures of life and the joys of living, who gets under your skin and who wants to get up close and personal. God is full of delight. God is sensual. God luxuriates in pleasure.

Meister Eckhart does not sound much like a conventional Christian. After all, if you are an unconventional Christian and you are going out for a night on the town, you probably wouldn't ask the heavenly father to go along. You wouldn't want to go out on the town with a God who might frown at you from time to time, clear his throat and say, "I'm not so sure I'd enjoy that so much if I were you."

I don't know about you, but I'd prefer to spend my night out on the town with a God who is voluptuous and delicious rather than judging and distant.

A God who is voluptuous and delicious seduces us into the beauty of life. The voluptuous Divine offers us an inexplicable gift when we open to life and get up close and personal. This God confirms what the mystics tell us, that God desires an erotic relationship with each of us and that if we in turn desire an erotic relationship with God, we will get it.

The word erotic comes from the Greek word *eros*, meaning "desire." When we hear the word *erotic* we are conditioned to think of its sexual connotations. It is true that sex is one aspect of the erotic, but it is only one. *Eros* is also the desire to be close, to be intimate, to share one's innermost self with another.

From the first taste of our mother's milk to our last breath, we are forever in search of an intimacy we can trust. This desire to open our innermost selves to others is deeply rooted. Our deepest need is to know others and be known ourselves. The universal human quest is to find not only someone but *someones* with whom we can fully share our lives.

Our souls are hungry to be in the presence of those who will listen without judging. Our souls long to be able to open to others who will understand and accept us unconditionally. What we all want is someone who will listen to us and sit with us in the silence. Innate in every human being is the desire to feel safe in the presence of another. As Parker Palmer puts it, "The soul is shy; the innermost self won't come out unless conditions are safe."[2]

We seek intimacy in many ways. We share tears and stories, we embrace, we open up, we give voice to our personal truths.

We are erotic by nature, and God is Eros with a capital E.

God is all heart. God is the breath of our breath, the life of our life. God is nearer to us than we are to ourselves. God is the inexplicable beauty of life.

It is a divine pleasure to feel close to everything that lives, moves and breathes. God is the mysterious vitality that fills us with that longing for belonging. The Divine energy within and among and beyond us is the source of all intimacies we share. The energy of intimacy is possible because the spirit of life lives in each and every one of us.

The psalmist wrote, "I sought God, and God answered me and delivered me from all my fears… O taste and see that God is good."[3]

Mostly we go through life settling for minor pleasures. It may be somewhat surprising to learn that the mystics, those spiritual giants, love pleasure. They often confess that they are nothing if not hedonistic. They say there is no greater pleasure than living in a state of intimacy with God. The more intimate you are with the Divine, the greater the pleasure.

It follows then that if God is in each of us, then one way to develop intimacy with the Holy Presence is by drawing close to other human beings. Taking this seriously could turn our world upside down. Taking this seriously would mean that life is transformed at every level. What if we opened up to Divine energy by seeing ourselves intimately related to one and all? Or what if the need for intimacy was recognized as a basic human right? We could write it into public policy.

Take the death penalty as an example. Capital punishment is an act of retribution, and retribution by its very nature is a violent act against intimacy. And I am especially struck by the fact that death row cases usually come down to a transaction between two people. I am not referring to the final interaction between the executioner and the prisoner, but rather to the relationship of the death row inmate and the person in government who hears the final appeal.

In that life and death situation, that person keeps his distance and considers the facts while sitting in his or her office.

The decision about whether someone should live or die based on words written on a piece of paper rather than on personal interaction with the human being whose life is at stake.

To make a life or death decision from a distance is too easy. What if the one who had the power of life and death over another had to come face to face with the person who is to be executed? Look into his or her eyes. See him or her up close. Listen first-hand to what the inmate has to say. For a brief while, share intimately in the life of that human being. It is one thing to deny clemency to a stranger, but it's altogether different to deny mercy to someone with whom you've developed some level of intimacy. Intimacy changes the way we see each other.

No one would think that having to make a life or death choice for someone by spending a few days eyeball-to-eyeball, heart-to-heart with them could be construed as pleasure in the sense of "having a fun time." But it would be pleasure in the sense of living with the Divine in intimacy and compassion. Most of us don't have the power to sign a death warrant. But I am convinced that in every moment of every day we do have other life and death powers over others. I do not mean this literally, of course. But we do have the power to choose to live close to others or to keep our distance. We don't usually meet people on death row, but in our everyday lives there is always someone who is looking for mercy.

We know this is true because every day we too are looking for mercy. A family member needs support and reassurance. A friend hopes that we will listen without judging. The grocery store clerk hopes that when we ask her how she is, we really care about her answer.

Experiencing closeness to another, even for just a moment, makes an immeasurable difference. Every day we need others to treat us with kindness and compassion. Every day we need to treat others with kindness and compassion. To embrace intimacy not only changes the way we feel about others, it changes the way we feel about ourselves. Ralph Waldo Emerson once said, "The gods we worship write their names on our faces, and a man will worship something... Therefore it behooves us to be careful what we are worshiping, for what we are worshiping we are becoming."[4]

It matters whether we worship a God of distance or a God of intimacy. An intimate God is at once transcendent and imminent, beyond and within. We live in the Divine and the Divine lives in us.

Angela of Foligno, a medieval mystic, put it eloquently when she wrote, "The eyes of my soul were opened, and I beheld the plenitude of God, wherein I did comprehend the whole world, both here and beyond the sea, and the abyss and ocean and all things. In all these things I beheld nothing but the divine power, in a manner assuredly indescribable; so that through excess of marveling the soul cried with a loud voice, saying, 'This whole world is full of God!'"[5]

We are living so near to the heart of God that we are in it, and it is in us. The gods we worship write their names on our faces.

The news of the day is full of horrible reports of people doing unspeakable things to others. The murder of young girls in an Amish school in Pennsylvania is one example. On the surface this story is godawful. That someone would enter a school and kill young girls is incomprehensible. But in that terrible narrative there were other stories.

After Charles Roberts took over that one-room school he told the girls he held there that he intended to kill them all.

When he announced his plans, 13-year-old Marian Fisher said, "Shoot me, and let the others go." She offered to give up her life so that her classmates could live.

But all the children were killed.

Amish families have a tradition of trying to embrace those who have hurt them. Several of the bereaved parents went to visit Charles Roberts' wife to do that. They also publicly announced that they forgave Charles Roberts. The God worshipped by Marian Fisher and those Amish parents was written on their faces.

Thomas Merton, the well-known Trappist monk, lived in a monastic community in Kentucky. One day, while in Louisville on a monastic errand, he suddenly had an epiphany. He wrote about it, saying, "I suddenly realized that I loved all the people and that none of them were or could be totally alien to me. As if waking from a dream, the dream of my separateness, of my 'special vocation' to be different."[6]

Waking up to a delicious and voluptuous God frees us from our dream of separateness and changes everything.

For a good time, call God.

---

[1] Matthew Fox, *Meditations with Meister Eckhart* (Bear and Company, 1983)
[2] Parker Palmer, *A Hidden Wholeness* (Jossey-Bass, 2004)
[3] Psalm 34:8
[4] Paul Brockelman, *Cosmology and Creation: The Spiritual Significance of Contemporary Cosmology* (New York: Oxford University Press, 1999) p. 115
[5] Eknath Easwaran, *Original Goodness* (Nilgiri Press, 1996)
[6] Robert Jingen Gunn, *Journeys into Emptiness: Dogen, Merton, Jung and the Quest for Transformation* (Paulist Press)

2

What Is the Soul?

The film comedian W. C. Fields was an ill-tempered man who hated religion. He hated Christmas Day and ironically died on Christmas Day in 1946. Several months before his death a friend paid him a visit. The friend was shocked to see W. C. Fields was propped up in bed, reading the Bible. The friend said, "Bill, I can't believe my eyes. You are reading the Bible. Why on earth are you reading the Bible?"

Fields replied, "I'm looking for loopholes."

We are all looking for loopholes, for ways to escape our mistakes and regrets. We live flawed lives and many of us are conditioned to believe that our imperfections can be traced to some fault with the soul.

The Christian doctrine of original sin implies that the soul is external to God. It implies that God creates souls in the same way an artist paints on a canvas. While the canvas holds the image the artist created, the picture itself is outside the artist. Though not a perfect analogy, the distinction between God as creator and soul as created sees the soul as separate from the Sacred. A work of art, to be sure, but the soul is outside of God.

In conventional Christianity, the soul is not only separate, but also corrupt. The Genesis story of Adam and Eve eating the forbidden fruit in the Garden of Eden is often used to explain how the human soul has been tainted from the very beginning. Adam and Eve's act of disobedience put a blot on their souls. They were evicted from the Garden and put out into the wilderness. Worse yet, being the literal parents of every human being since then meant that every baby born into the world was born with a blot on its soul. To put it bluntly, this means that the soul is a stranger, alien to God. This is the essence of what conventional Christianity teaches about the soul.

Every religion has its creation myths, but those in the Abrahamic traditions, or desert religions, consistently view God as a stranger and human beings as alienated from their Source.

There is a Sufi creation story that presents a different version of creation and the soul. The Sufis say the soul was created because God was lonely and desired to be loved. So God said, "I will separate souls from myself and send them away (note that the soul is originally *a part* of God rather than being created by God) for a while so that when they return they will be bubbling with the intensity of love."

The souls went out into time and space and were sustained by Divine light and the heavenly vibration. The soul is thus forever stirred by this music of the spheres. That which empowers the soul is of God and from God. Being of the same essence of God, the soul innately and unconsciously longs to return. Ultimately, every drop returns to the ocean. The soul is a drop of consciousness in the ocean of God.[1]

So how is your soul in this very moment? Would you know? Have you ever seen it? Have you ever touched it? What does a soul look like?

Walk through a bookstore, thumb through a magazine, read through the announcements of conferences and seminars with titles like *Healing the Wounds of the Soul*, *The Care of the Soul*, *Ways to Keep Your Soul Alive*, to name but a few, and we see what a popular topic the soul is these days.

Practically everyone has an opinion on what the soul is or is not, what it needs and how to heal it. Books for and about the soul are bestsellers. After publishing the first four volumes of *Chicken Soup for the Soul*, the authors diversified. There was *Chicken Soup for the Christian Soul*, *Chicken Soup for the Teenage Soul*, *Chicken Soup for the Mother's Soul*, among others. How many different kinds of souls are there?

Chicken soup for the sick soul comes in many forms: as religion, as psychotherapy, as a new relationship if we find that "special someone." We are perpetually in search of a cure-all. Promise me a panacea!

The Secret is currently being offered up as a cure for the sick soul. *The Secret* promises to transform your life. It promises to be a magic potion or a silver bullet. Just think positive thoughts about what we want and we'll get it.

I happen to believe there is something to the law of attraction and the power of positive thinking. But no matter how positive the vibes are that you put out, the world will bring you things you never asked for. After seeing the DVD and reading the book, one woman said to me, "I've been trying to live by the law of attraction, but it doesn't seem to be working."

Life is disillusioning and this is a good thing. The spiritual journey is the quest for Truth with a capital T. This requires the courage to live beneath the surface illusions that divert our attention from the deeper truths within. So many "spiritual programs" promise quick remedies. But when we live from our depths rather than our shallows, we discover that spiritual life is something more than simply getting what we want. The purpose of spirituality is to connect us to our true essence, the true self, often referred to as the soul.

The soul represents our core, our essence, our true self. But are we simply making this up? Is the soul a figment of our imagination? I know of no one capable of producing evidence to verify its existence. The soul cannot be seen under a microscope or detected by a CT scan.

Whatever the soul is or isn't, most would agree that it is not a physical or material "thing" capable of being held or grasped. Its mass cannot be weighed or quantified. Its existence cannot be proven or refuted by logic or reason. We know the soul intuitively by encountering it. The soul is spirit. It is ethereal.

A number of years ago, Annie Dillard was in Chicago to give a talk on her book *For the Time Being*. During the talk, she said she believed in God. During the question period that followed, a man asked her how someone as bright and knowledgeable as she obviously was could possibly believe in God. She paused and said, "Well, we've met."

No one could challenge her. Her experience of God was not something that could be measured or verified. She knew God because she had met God. She believed because she had her own experience. Likewise with the soul – it can only be met personally and intuitively.

The mystics unanimously agree that the soul is that deep and inexplicable part of ourselves that gives us the power to become larger than life. As a minister, I have sat with many people who have died. Several moments after they have taken their last breath, I often find myself staring at the lifeless body asking, "Where did you go?"

A living, breathing human being can seem larger than life. A dead body appears to be smaller, a hollow shell. The vitality of being alive gives the body a larger presence.

The soul is *who* we are and *how* we are connected to life. It is the source of our deepest yearning and the promise of our greatest fulfillment. It is the key that can open us to life's greater mystery and meaning. When this life force withdraws, the cadaver shrinks and appears smaller.

Nasrudin is a Sufi character of medieval origin. There is a Nasrudin story that tells of how one night he was crawling around outside his house on his hands and knees under a lantern when a friend walked up and asked him what he was doing. Continuing to scour the ground without looking up, Nasrudin answered, "I have lost my key and I am looking for it."

So his friend got down on his hands and knees and joined Nasrudin in scooping up dirt, looking for the lost key. After a while, the friend stood up and said, "Nasrudin, where exactly did you lose the key?"

Nasrudin replied, "Oh, I lost it in the house."

"Then why," his friend implored, "are we looking for it out here?"

"Because the light is so much better out here," smiled Nasrudin.

For many years I kept coming back to this story. I even used it in a sermon or two. But it wasn't until I began to find and explore my soul that I got a deeper meaning from it.

In the late 1980s, my marriage of many years ended in divorce. It was an excruciating experience. During the early days of that ordeal my psyche was ablaze with pain. The nights were long and agonizing. I couldn't sleep, think or work. One long night when the pain was especially intense and I ached from head to toe, I wondered if I could survive the night. I have never known such a combination of physical and mental pain. Curled up in a fetal position, I lay in the darkness. My eyes were closed.

As I looked into my inner darkness, the pain in my gut reached an excruciating peak. Certain I was bleeding from the belly, I brushed the sheets with my hand. The sheets were dry. Gradually a ring of light appeared in my darkness and I heard a voice, not with my ears, but in my heart. I heard, "Do not be afraid. You are not alone. You have never been alone. You will never be alone."

That experience was at once compelling, powerful and consoling. Intuitively I knew then, and I believe now, that I was seeing the light of my own soul. Intuitively, I knew then, as I do now, that God was speaking to me through the soul.

This encounter unlocked a spiritual door I didn't know existed and led me to pay attention to the mystics. Eventually I discovered Saint Teresa of Avila's *The Interior Castle*. The soul, Teresa said, is like an interior castle, a huge and magnificent dwelling. In Mirabai Starr's warm and accessible translation of *The Interior Castle* are these words from Teresa, "No one else controls access to this perfect place. Give yourself your own unconditional permission to go there. Absolve yourself of missing the mark again and again. Believe the incredible truth that the Beloved has chosen for his dwelling place the core of your own being because that is the single most beautiful place in all of creation. Waste no time. Enter the center of your soul."

In the culmination of *The Interior Castle*, Teresa writes, "It is impossible to say anything more that could be understood with words, except that the soul, I mean the spirit of this soul, is made one with God."[2]

Within us is an interior castle where God dwells. We don't have to look outside where we think the light is better. God is met in the center of the soul. In a sermon called *Where the Soul Is, There Is God*, Meister Eckhart said, "God lives in the soul with everything that he and all creatures are. Therefore, where the soul is, there God is, for the soul is in God."[3]

As we begin to uncover and enter our interior castle, we soon discover that it is indeed the dwelling place of God and a source of infinite strength. My meditation teacher and contemporary mystic Sant Rajinder Singh put it, "Within us lies the unlimited power and energy of the soul. Tapping into it can enrich and transform us. Its rich qualities include fearlessness, immortality, connectedness, unconditional love and bliss."[4]

Ralph Waldo Emerson said, "Within us is the soul of the whole, the wise silence, the universal beauty, to which every part and particle is equally related; the eternal One. When it breaks through our intellect, it is genius; when it breaks through our will, it is virtue; when it flows through our affections, it is love."[5]

The mystics challenge us not to believe in second-hand spiritual truth. Don't believe it just because it's been handed down. Don't believe it simply because others say it is true. Don't believe it because the mystics say it's true. Let your experience be your teacher, trust yourself. Open up and allow the wisdom of your own soul to spill into your consciousness. Why look outside when we know it is really inside?

If you are scheduled for major surgery you will naturally want to choose a surgeon who has had experience performing the surgery. When it comes to working on our own souls would we expect any less? We do not want to hear about our souls from someone who has mere theoretical information. Speculation has a place but it is nothing compared to actual experience. A mystic is like an experienced surgeon of the soul. Through spiritual practices such as meditation or centring prayer, mystics clear away the debris covering their interior castle and show us how to enter the interior castle in us.

Great spiritual teachers, past and present, live at a level of soul awareness. In his book *Meeting Jesus Again for the First Time*, Marcus Borg says that someone who lives at this level of soul awareness is a "spirit person." Borg says that Jesus was a spirit person, and that always there have been spirit persons on the earth. The term spirit person can be used interchangeably with mystic. These are people for whom the soul is no longer a mere idea and God no longer an abstract concept. This is not to say they know everything or understand all things, but simply that the meaning, direction and purpose of their lives and of life is no longer a question mark.

When we listen to or read about mystics, it's true that *we* are relying on second-hand information. But at least they speak of what they have directly experienced rather than the latest collective guess. They do not tell us to place our ultimate trust in the pope, the Bible, doctrine, or anything external. They tell us that the truth awaits us within us. They speak out of empirical awareness.

The mystics say that these inexplicable and unimaginable experiences don't come from outer space but from inner space. They tell us there is a spark of God in each and every one of us. Even in the conventional Christian tradition there are hints that this divine light lives in all. In John's Gospel, Jesus said, "I am the light of the world."[6]

As a mystic, as a spirit person, Jesus beheld the splendour of the light of God shining from his soul. And then, in Matthew's Gospel, in the Sermon on the Mount, Jesus, turns to the multitude on the hill and says, "You are the light of the world."[7]

As a spirit person, a mystic, Jesus could see the one light of God in all.

The soul is of God and from God. Like the Holy One, it is always whole, peaceful, and blissful. No matter how the soul is covered by suffering, the soul's integrity is always intact. The soul's immune system is perfect. It is fearless, boundless and eternal. It is that deepest part of us that recognizes the unity of all things. The soul is the innermost heart. It is perfect and pure love.

In this life we all have our ups and downs. We all pass through the valley of the shadow of death at some point. Sometimes we fall into the abyss of pain or struggle through the quicksand of despair. But the soul is never wounded. It is the eternal source of wholeness within us, waiting to be uncovered. Whenever we experience healing, connection and wholeness, the soul is rising up into our consciousness.

No matter how low we drop, eventually we will rise up. No matter how much pain we have, we will get through it. No matter how bad it gets, the soul is eternally resilient. The soul, the Spirit, is immutable and indestructible because the centre of the soul is God, and God is love.

Perhaps you too have experienced this Truth: Love is stronger even than death. This is the soul's quiet voice speaking to and through us.

1   Darshan Singh, *The Secret of Secrets* (Sawan Kirpal Publications, 1978)
2   Mirabai Starr, *The Interior Castle: A New Translation* (River Books, 2003)
3   Matthew Fox, *Breakthrough: Meister Eckhart's Creation Spirituality* (Image Books, 1980)
4   Rajinder Singh, *The Silken Thread of the Divine* (S. K. Publications, 2005)
5   Elbert Hubbard, ed., *The Essential Writings of Ralph Waldo Emerson* (Kessenger Publishing, 2005)
6   John 8:12
7   Matthew 5:14

3

Soul Liberty

··· ✥ ···

A large family moved to a new city. The family had seven children. This family had a very difficult time finding a landlord who would rent to them. Every time they found a suitable apartment, the landlord was hesitant to rent to so large a family.

After several days of fruitless searching, the father asked the mother to take the four younger children to visit the cemetery. He then took the three older children and set out on another day of apartment hunting. After looking most of the morning, they found a place that was just right.

Then the landlord asked the usual question: "How many children do you have?"

The father answered, "Ah well, seven. But four are with their dear mother in the cemetery."

They got the apartment.

You could say the father wasn't telling the whole truth. But he was telling the truth. So what does it mean to tell the truth?

We raise our children to tell the truth. We take oaths promising to tell the truth, nothing but the whole truth, so help me God. When a person is accused of a crime the prosecutor will try to punch holes in the defendant's story and bring out the contradictions. If the defendant contradicts himself, by implication he is not telling the truth. The truth, we are told, is seamless.

"Truth is my authority, not some authority my truth," said Anne Hutchinson, a 17th-century American pioneer of religious freedom. She was then declared an "American Jezebel who had gone a-whoring from God" and brought to trial. She was found guilty of heresy in 1637. Her accusers said her truth was false and theirs was true.

What is the truth and who has the authority to decide?

Even at a mundane level, what is true for one person is not necessarily true for another. We go to a movie with friends. After the credits roll, we walk out of the theatre and one friend says the movie was fabulous. Another says it was okay, but not great. We say we hated that movie and that we found it depressing. Who is right? Who is wrong? What is the truth?

It depends on where we stand.

Religious evangelicals and fundamentalists say there is one truth and it can be known in only one way. It's my way or the highway. If I think that my beliefs are true and you believe the opposite, then what you believe must be false.

One day at a meeting in my office, it came up that my associate minister and I were vegetarians. At that point, another person in the meeting began making jokes about vegetarians and confessed that he was a rabid carnivore. He was living a carnivore truth and could not imagine how anyone could possibly choose vegetarian truth. He admitted he was not comfortable with our vegetarian orientation.

We moved on to other topics and finished the meeting. Getting up, he looked down at the sofa. He lit up as if he had just made a great discovery. Pointing to the sofa he said, "Aha! Wait a minute! Isn't this a leather sofa? How do you explain this? How do you account for this inconsistency? A vegetarian with a leather sofa!"

He grinned ear to ear, certain that he'd nailed my hypocrisy.

Then a quote from Walt Whitman came to me and I said, "Do I contradict myself? Very well, I contradict myself (I am large for I contain multitudes)."[1]

We laughed.

The truth is one and there are many versions of it. There is something of the truth in all of us, but none of us has it all.

From this insight comes the concept of soul liberty. Soul liberty is the freedom to seek the truth in one's own way, according to one's own conscience.[2] Also known as the "right of private judgment," soul liberty is the conviction that human freedom is not simply a matter of individual rights or even one of human dignity. The soul's quest for truth is a birthright given by God to every human being.

But the most important thing about soul liberty is that it allows us to acknowledge that the spiritual journey is fraught with ambiguity. It is a God-given right to be wrong. If we are wrong today, maybe we will get it right tomorrow. If we are right today, we may be wrong tomorrow. Soul liberty does not provide a complete shrink-wrapped package of behavioural norms.

There is a story about some students who went to their rabbi with an argument about who was right and who was wrong.

The first one said, "Rabbi, is it not true that the path to God is built on effort and energy?"

The second disciple strenuously disagreed. "It is not about effort," he said. "You can't find God unless you get rid of your ego."

The more they argued, the more obvious their differences became. The rabbi sat and listened with perfect attentiveness. Finally, the first disciple turned to the rabbi.

"Am I not right?" he asked. "Is not the way to God built on effort and energy, upon keeping the law? Rabbi, isn't this the truth path?"

The rabbi answered, "Yes, of course you are correct."

The second student became visibly shaken and launched into an eloquent argument for believing in the path of surrender and letting go. Concluding his brilliant speech, he looked earnestly into the eyes of the rabbi and asked: "Is not this the truth path?"

And again the rabbi answered, "Yes, of course you are right."

A third student who had been sitting silent suddenly jumped up and said, "But master, they can't both be right."

To which the rabbi smiled and said, "Of course, you are also right."[3]

Soul liberty implies that no one has all of the truth but all of us have some part of it.

Soul liberty is the freedom to seek the truth without fear of coercion or repression. In social and political terms, it is the freedom to choose where you want to go, do what you want to do (within certain agreed social and political constraints) and be who you want to be. Freedom includes the belief that individuals are endowed with the inalienable right of autonomy.

But spiritual freedom is not the same thing as social and political freedom.

In his *Epistle to the Galatians*, Paul writes, "For freedom, Christ has set you free. Do not submit again to the yoke of slavery."[4]

A slave is someone who is completely dependent upon somebody else for their very existence. One consequence of this dependency is that the slave loses his or her capacity to choose. They must do as they are told or lose their source of livelihood.

Spiritually speaking, if we depend on anything in the external world to give us inner security, we have submitted to the yoke of slavery. It is often easier to become a slave to somebody else's version of the truth than to have to search for our own. I have known many who have become slaves to their religion's orthodoxy. They are dependent on a single version of truth or a literal belief in the Bible or unquestioning loyalty to doctrine to supply their spiritual truths. Whether it is our religious belief, job, money, family, or friends, if we believe that something external will give us security, it is potentially a slave master.

To put aside our external dependencies and experience spiritual freedom requires a radical openness to the God who lives in the centre of the soul. Opening to this inner teacher is not something that happens overnight. Sometimes we think we are getting a clear message or direction from within only to learn later that we were wrong. But with daily spiritual practice, we learn to become attentive to this inner light. Daily spiritual practice helps us put our attention within.

Attention is the outward expression of the soul. What we do with our attention enslaves or liberates the soul. Professor Diana Eck writes, "I was well into my twenties before I paid attention to attention. It was an itinerant Zen teacher who came to Cambridge in the early 1970s who told the tale of the Japanese Zen Master Ikkyu, an eccentric teacher who was approached by a serious student and asked about the main teachings of Zen Buddhism. Ikkyu took a brush and wrote out the Japanese word for "attention." Thinking this to be too brief, the student asked for the teacher to write something more. He took his brush and wrote, "Attention, attention." When pressed for something additional, he took out his brush and wrote, "Attention, attention, attention."[5]

In every waking moment of every day, our attention goes to something. Wherever it goes, we go there too. This is why the question of where we put our attention is spiritual and crucial. The mystics tell us that our problem is not that we are original sinners, but original sleepers. It is only when we pay attention to where we are putting our attention that we begin to wake up.

The practice of meditation is placing our attention within ourselves, where God is. Teresa of Avila called this recollecting the soul. One recollects the soul by pulling together the scattered attention and gathering it within. If we practise this over time, our attention becomes less scattered. As we gather our attention, we wake up to God within the soul. We wake up to God when the rambling, scattered mind is stilled. This is the work of a lifetime.

On the surface, soul liberty is about the integrity of the individual human being and the cultivation of conscience. At a deeper level, soul liberty is the intention to take our attention from life's broken surface to a deeper truth. The ultimate purpose of soul liberty is to awaken us to what Thomas Merton called, "the hidden wholeness beneath the broken surface."

Connecting to and living out of the treasure of the soul is not narcissistic. It's just the opposite. We can only see the ineffable light of God in others once we see it in ourselves.

And wherever and whenever and in whoever this light appears, it is the same light. One light appears in all. We are given the freedom to choose to see the Divine embodied everywhere.

This is the one Truth that puts all our other truths in perspective. This is the one Truth that is powerful enough to set us free.

1   Walt Whitman, *Song of Myself*, sct. 51, *Leaves of Grass* (1855)
2   Mass moments.com, *Roger Williams Banished* (Massachusetts Foundation for the Humanities, October 9, 2005)
3   Feldman and Kornfield, *Stories of the Spirit, Stories of the Heart* (HarperCollins, 1991) p. 307
4   Galatians 5:1
5   Diana Eck, *Encountering God: From Bozeman to Banaras* (Beacon Press, 1993)

4

Finding God by Subtraction

I have long lived by the axiom that it is better to remain silent and appear a fool than to open my mouth and remove all doubt. Who among us hasn't had the experience of saying something, only to recoil instantly, thinking, "I don't believe I said that! I feel like such a fool."

In his book *Jacob the Baker*, Noah Ben Shea tells the story of the fool who went to see the king. As the fool walked along the road to the king's palace, people pointed and jeered at him and shouted, "What makes you think a person like you can go to see the king?"

"Well," answered the fool, "I'm going to be the king's teacher."

When the fool said this, the people doubled over in laughter. Some of them laughed so hard they couldn't stand up.

Word reached the king that the fool was on his way. The king decided he would end this nonsense quickly, so he had the fool brought immediately to the royal court. Sitting back on his throne he asked, "Why do you dare to disturb the king?"

"I come to be the royal teacher," answered the fool in a very matter of fact manner.

The king laughed. "How can a fool teach me?"

"You see," said the fool, "you are already asking me questions."

Silence fell over the court. The king gathered himself and stared at this ridiculous person standing in front of him.

"Well, you've offered me a clever response. But you have not answered my questions!"

"Only a fool has all the answers," said the fool with great humility.

The king was clearly losing ground and he began to sputter. "But what would others say if they knew the king had a fool for a teacher?"

The fool stood silent. Dropping his head in respect, he said, "Better to have a fool for a teacher than a fool for a king."

Humbled, the king said, "Now it is I who feels like a fool."[1]

It is only a fool who has never felt like one.

Of all the species in creation, the feeling of foolishness is unique to the human being. From presidents to paupers, from royalty to the lowest rung of the social ladder, we all know what it's like to feel a fool. A Welsh proverb points out that if every fool wore a crown, then we all would be kings and queens.

Mainly we are accidental fools. We trip ourselves up. We say the wrong thing at the wrong time. We zig when we should zag, we jump ahead when we should hold back. We all know what it feels like to have, as they say, egg on our face.

There is also a deeper foolishness and it can hit us between the eyes when we least expect it. This is the foolishness that comes not because of something we've said or done, but because there is nothing to say or do. This kind of foolishness reminds us that we really don't know anything. No matter what we say, no matter what we do, it is of no consequence. We don't know what to say because there is nothing to say.

There are moments in life that are so poignant that the only thing we can do is to let the silence speak. This is God by subtraction. This is the wordless Presence. This is the less that is more.

This happened to Liz with her 60-year-old friend Marge. Marge had arthroscopy performed on her knee, and Liz told her she would pay her a visit the day after surgery. Liz showed up and pressed the buzzer to Marge's apartment. No answer. She pressed it again and again. No answer. Eventually Liz found someone with a key. Together they entered Marge's apartment and found her dead on the floor next to the telephone.

When Liz found her friend Marge she was stunned and speechless. She froze at the sight of her dead friend's body. She didn't know what to say or do.

In our culture silence is viewed not as a teacher but as a problem. Henri Nouwen puts it like this. "One of our main problems is that in this chatty society, silence has become a very fearful thing. For most people, silence creates itchiness and nervousness. Many experience silence not as full and rich but empty and hollow. For them silence is like a gaping abyss which can swallow them up."[2]

The impulse in our culture is to avoid the awkward silence. We leap to fill the gaps and deny the ambiguity. The problem with this response is that life *is* ambiguous. Things happen that leave us speechless. Unexpected experiences overtake us. Every now and then something happens that turns our lives inside out and we don't know what to say or think about it.

Shortly after becoming a newly minted reverend at age 25, I received a call to my first church in a small town in eastern Kansas. One month after my arrival, a 95-year-old woman died and it was time to perform my first funeral. As was the custom, the family had the casket open not only during the visitation, but also throughout the service. And I remember that it felt simply weird to stand behind a podium in a funeral home in the presence of this elderly body in a casket. But because I had requested the advice of a few seasoned ministers about what to say, I managed to speak the appropriate words without difficulty. It was easier because the deceased had lived a long and productive life. It was her time.

Six months later I faced a deeper challenge. A 25-year-old man who had been in an accident lay in a hospital bed in a coma. His young wife sat weeping next to the bed. I sat beside her. I didn't know what to say. I had thought that as an ordained minister with a Master of Divinity degree I would know what to do. But I didn't. I just sat there beside them.

I kept showing up, day after day, feeling utterly incompetent. I held his limp hand, held her frightened hand and occasionally said a prayer.

Of course, I hadn't learned any prayers in seminary for such an occasion so I would say something like, "God, we don't know what to say. But please comfort Vickie and work with the doctors as instruments of your healing for Gary."

I prayed this prayer every time I paid a visit. As soon as the words left my lips, I felt hollow, ridiculous. What could I possibly say in the presence of this tragedy?

Two weeks after my first visit, Gary died.

The day of the funeral, I stood with the widow by the casket. When she talked about the darkness in her, I felt like I was in it too. When she said she was falling into an abyss, I embraced her. I felt completely helpless.

But it was there, standing beside a casket with a grieving widow, that I learned a priceless lesson, one untaught and unavailable in seminary. I learned that the power of being present is the greatest power we human beings possess.

What matters most is not what we say. It is not what we believe or think we know. It is not speaking the right words or offering blessed assurance. What matters most is our capacity to be present with what is, and our simple entering and sharing the mysterious and ambiguous silence. God by subtraction.

When everything is at stake, when life itself hangs in the balance, and when we are facing the truth of what is, words become mere background noise. In life's defining moments, what gets through to us is the caring and compassionate presence of others. The Quakers say, "If you can't improve on the silence, then don't speak."

This practice of silence is central to the spiritual life.

There is a story about a fifth-century monk who lived in a cloistered community. His spiritual life was a mess. He felt troubled, distracted and unfulfilled. So the monk went to the abbot to ask for a teaching, hoping to hear something that would help him go forward in his spiritual journey.

"Please give me a word," implored the monk. "Tell me something that will inspire and motivate me."

The abbot answered, "Go and sit in silence in your cell. The silence will teach you everything."

I learned long ago that often it is best to let the silence speak. The silence reminds us that we are big fat fools and there is nothing to do but to open ourselves to God within, among and around us.

Habakkuk is one of the minor prophets in the Judeo/Christian tradition. The book of Habakkuk in the Hebrew Bible is a scant three chapters, but it tells a big story. In it, Habakkuk protests, complains and is upset with God because God allows horrible things to happen. Why does God allow bad things to happen to good people? Why does terror so often swallow up goodness? Habakkuk wants answers.

God does answer Habakkuk and it is not the answer Habakkuk expects. God tells Habakkuk that no matter how bad things get, and no matter how upset he is, there is only one thing he needs to know. God's answer is that "The Lord is in the Holy Temple, let all the earth keep silence."[3]

The world within and the world without is a cacophony of noise. In our minds there is constant chatter and the ticker tape rattle of our own restless thoughts. The inner noise echoes the outer racket. The outer clatter mirrors the inner commotion.

Where is the silent and holy temple in which God resides?

The holy temple is life itself and silence is found in the soul. The whole universe is God's temple. Let all the earth confront its foolishness and keep silence.

The universal God is always present. Divine Presence is encountered when the soul rests in silence. Just as the body requires rest to restore its energy, so the soul requires silence to awaken to its own Truth. If we don't empty ourselves of noise then our lives become the noise. Silence gives the soul a Sabbath. Silence gives us rest.

Chuang Tzu, the early interpreter of Taoism, tells the story of a man who was so disturbed by the sight of his own shadow and so displeased with his own footsteps that he determined to get rid of both. The method he hit upon was to run away from them. So he got up and ran. But every time he put his foot down he created another step, and his shadow kept up to him without the slightest difficulty. He attributed his failure to escape to the fact that he was not running fast enough. So he ran faster and faster, without stopping, until he finally dropped dead.

The man in the story failed to realize that if he merely stepped into the shade, his shadow would vanish, and if he sat down and stayed still, there would be no more footsteps. To open to silence is to stop running and step into the shade. In silence we begin to hear the still small voice.

The practice of silence teaches us how to be quiet within even when the world is bustling without. Learning to sit in silence, either alone or with others, practising meditation or contemplative prayer, and learning to feel comfortable with awkward silences in our everyday conversations are all skills that require practice. Opening to our interior silence is an acquired skill. We may make all kinds of noise, but the Divine lives in silence.

Contemplative prayer comes from a deep place of stillness and quiet. When the mind is quiet the still small voice speaks.

But what does it say?

It says that we are beloved. It tells us that inextricably and eternally, you are "my beloved."

When people fall in love, just being in love and being with one's beloved is all that one needs. Under the influence of the still small voice we find ourselves in the presence of the Divine Beloved. Captivated by Divine presence, everything looks different.

We all have our attachments. We all have our expectation and ideas of how life is supposed to be. We are attached to how we want things to work out. But the still small voice whispers to us that what we have today will be gone tomorrow. It tells us softly to let it go. Let it all go. Let it all go.

Speaking out of this still small voice, Quaker Etta May wrote,

If (you) need
Anything and cannot
    Find it,
Just come to me
    And I'll tell you
How to get along
    Without it.[4]

The still small voice says, "You are my beloved. This is all you need and all you need to know. You can get along without everything else."

Be quiet and let go.

Nikos Kazantzakis put it like this: "I have one longing only… to discover behind the visible and unceasing stream of the world an invisible and immutable presence is hiding…and 'what is my duty?… to let the mind fall silent that I may hear the invisible calling.'"[5]

And this is why Meister Eckhart said, "God is not attained by a process of addition to anything in the soul, but by a process of subtraction."[6]

1   Noah Ben Shea, *Jacob the Baker* (Villard Books, 1989)
2   Henri Nouwen, *Seeds of Hope: A Henri Nouwen Reader* (Image Books, 1997) p. 56
3   Habakkuk 2:20
4   Doris Grumbach, *The Presence of Absence* (Beacon Press 1998)
5   Nikos Kazantzakis, *The Saviors of God: Spiritual Exercises* (Simon and Schuster, 1969)
6   James Clark and John V. Skinner, *Meister Eckhart: Selected Treatises and Sermons Translated from Latin and German with an Introduction and Notes* (London: Faber & Faber Ltd, 1958) p. 194

5

Do You Believe in Divine Intervention?

O ne day, that Sufi rascal, Nasrudin,[1] was throwing handfuls of bread crumbs around his house.

"What are you doing?" asked his neighbour.

"Keeping the tigers away," answered Nasrudin.

"But Nasrudin, there are no tigers in these parts."

"That's right!" says Nasrudin. "That's proof the crumbs work!"

So, what is the truth? Did Nasrudin's bread crumbs keep the tigers away? Or did he simply believe what he wanted to believe?

Several days after hurricane Katrina struck the Gulf coast of the United States, a story was published in *USA Today* about Edward and Bettina Larsen and their three children, who had sailed their boat to the Florida Keys. As hurricane warnings were posted, the Larsen's friends became concerned that they hadn't returned to home port and notified the Coast Guard.

The Coast Guard started a search, but high winds and rough seas forced them to call it off.

A day after the storm had passed, the Coast Guard resumed the search and miraculously spotted the family of five stranded near their beached boat on a mangrove island 16 miles out to sea. One by one, the family members were hoisted into a Coast Guard helicopter and then they were all taken safely home.

Commenting on the rescue, a family friend said, "Sometimes there is a thing called Divine intervention."

Divine intervention. Mere coincidence, good fortune or fate? It depends on how you look at it.

Shortly after hurricane Katrina's rampage, a terrorist website proclaimed that, "the hurricane was a Divine sign against the corrupt crusading America. The hurricane should be taken as a warning to America that even with its military force and technology, nothing can be done to thwart the power of Allah, who guides humanity as he sees fit."

In other words, God created the hurricane as punishment, like the flood and the destruction of Sodom and Gomorrah. So Divine intervention creates suffering for some and joy for others. Go figure.

Some saved from the storm believe they were saved by an act of Divine intervention. Some claim the storm itself was Divine intervention in the form of punishment. What we see depends on where we stand. Does God interfere or intervene? Does the Divine alter the course of people's lives or change the direction of history?

Most people I know would like to believe in a Divine intervention that takes a positive form, as in answered prayer.

When we say that God has answered our prayers, we usually mean we got what they asked for. On the other hand, if we don't get what we pray for, maybe God is simply saying no!

And then there's another point of view that says good and bad things happen because that's just the way life is. God has nothing to do with it.

In his Pulitzer Prize-winning novel *The Bridge of San Luis Rey*, Thornton Wilder writes about an 18th-century Peruvian village located near a bridge. This bridge spanned a high gulf in the mountains and hundreds of travellers crossed over it every day.

One day, Catholic monk Brother Juniper stopped to wipe his forehead and gaze upon "the screen of snowy peaks in the distance, then into the gorge below him, filled with plumage of dark green trees and green birds. He felt at peace. Then his glance fell upon the bridge, and at that moment a twanging noise filled the air, as when the string of some musical instrument snaps… and he saw the bridge divide and swing, throwing the people into the valley below.

"Immediately the thought occurred to Brother Juniper, 'Why did this thing happen to those five people?' At that instant he resolved to investigate the lives of the five victims."

In the end, Brother Juniper concluded that of those five people, none was any better or worse than the other. None was more religious, more righteous. They were all good, well-meaning people.

"Why those five people?" Brother Juniper asks. "Why not some Divine intervention to keep them from stepping on that bridge?"

I was six years old and sitting at the breakfast table when my parents told me a story I remember to this day. The day before, my aunt Juanita had gone to the train station and just as she stepped aboard, her youngest son, Randy, began to cry out. Somehow my aunt had kissed Randy's two older brothers goodbye but not him. Stepping back from the train, she hurried to Randy and gave him a long hug. She turned around and saw that the train was moving out of the station. She ran after it but couldn't catch it.

It so happened that the train she missed later crashed, killing scores of the people on board.

In my family, this story became proof of Divine intervention. A few of my relatives even insisted that God caused my cousin Randy to cry out so that his mother would miss the train.

In situations such as these, it is natural to wonder why some people are spared while others die. Belief in Divine intervention is based on the premise that God is an activist. The word intervention implies that God steps into the events of our lives and acts. And by projecting our egos and attributes onto God, we make God in our image. So by its very nature, Divine intervention requires belief in a person-like being who thinks the way we think. It requires a belief in a personal God.

Woody Allen once quipped, "If only God would give me some clear sign! Like making a large deposit in my name at a Swiss bank."

Many people, it seems, bank on God to give them special treatment. However, I do not believe that God is at my beck and call to answer my prayers or do what I think needs to be done.

I do not believe in a personal God. The God I've met is impersonal or transpersonal. A transpersonal God does not seek out individuals by bestowing favor on some while turning away from others. A transpersonal God is always here, always there, always everywhere. The Holy One does not seek me out personally, but if I climb out of my self-absorption I can wake up to the experience of Divine Presence.

Asking for Divine intervention is to ask a person-like God-being to come to the rescue. Whenever I hear people jubilantly tell me that God has intervened, performed a miracle, saved them from death, I understand the momentary bliss. But our deepest need is not for Divine intervention but for Divine Presence. We need the experience of an enduring presence that lasts an eternity far more than an intervention that lasts a few moments.

God is not far from each one of us, for in God we live and move and have our being.[2]

If we dive into the ocean for a swim, we will get wet. The wetness of the ocean is a personal experience. But the ocean doesn't come looking for us. It is vast, available and accessible, but it does not seek us out. It's just there if we decide we want to get wet. This is not a perfect metaphor, but it moves us in the right direction.

It has not been my experience that God appears in my life like a pop-up on my computer screen, magically appearing between me and my difficulties in order to blow them away. My experience has been quite the opposite. I have endured pain, grief, and hard times and it was obvious that God did not step in at these times to make things better. It is not that God was absent. It's rather that God is a different kind of Presence.

God did not intervene between me and my manic episode some years ago. God did not intervene between my car and the fellow that hit it, totalling the car and breaking my ribs. God has not intervened in my life in order to make it pain free, and, looking back, I see this was a good thing. Divine intervention that saves us from pain would not be an aid to spiritual growth.

It would be quite the opposite. Wanting a way out and praying for an intervention are defences against facing ourselves and what is really going on in our lives.

So many people want a sugar daddy God. We want someone to bail us out, change our circumstances or defend us. We want a never-failing bulwark, God the mighty fortress.

I talk to a lot of people whose lives are in upheaval. They would like God to defend them against pain, suffering, and uncertainty. But they know this isn't realistic. So usually when people come in to talk to me about what is happening in their lives, they do not expect intervention or protection. They come because they need someone to listen to them and to be present with them. They need to sit with someone who will hear them without judgment. They need a witness.

I am often amazed that they say they feel better when they leave. I'm amazed because I haven't really done anything except to be as present as possible.

This is something we can all do for our friends and family. We can be open, present, and compassionate even if we can't intervene to change any particular situation. We can be like a spacious ocean of love for each other in whatever situation we find ourselves.

Compassionate presence is both mystery and miracle. It changes nothing, yet it changes everything.

Rabbi Abraham Joshua Heschel[3] calls this need for Divine Presence Divine pathos, meaning that we human beings have an innate sympathy for God. One might even say we are heartsick for God. We are heartsick and homesick.

What we long for is not simply a presence that keeps us from facing life or one that will change the current unpleasant situation. What we really long for is a presence that helps us to outshine whatever difficulty we are in. What we really long for is an eternal presence that will change us, regardless of the circumstances.

The most astonishing truth is that this Divine Presence is available and accessible to everyone all of the time. But waking up to it is another thing altogether.

In her stunning little book *The Presence of Absence*, Doris Grumbach writes about an experience she had as a young woman in the late 1940s.

Many years ago an extraordinary thing happened to me. I have never been able to forget it. I have tried to believe it did not happen. But the memory of it, nagging, persistent, unavoidable, has never left me. It was a simple thing: I sat on the shallow steps of a small house we owned north of New York City. My husband had taken our two, very young children (for an outing). I was alone, for me a rare condition. I do not remember thinking about anything in particular in that hour except perhaps how pleasant, in my noisy life, how agreeable the silence was.

What happened was this: sitting there, almost squatting on those wooden steps, listening to the quiet, I was filled with a unique feeling of peace, an impression so intense that it seemed to expand into ineffable joy, a huge delight. It went on second after second, so pervasive that it seemed to fill my entire body. I relaxed into it, luxuriated in it. Then with no warning...I felt, with a certainty I cannot account for, a sense of the presence of God.

You cannot know how extraordinary this was unless you understand that I was a young woman without a history of belief, without a formal religion or any faith at all...But more astonishing to me, at that moment, was that I identified, without a moment's doubt, Whose presence it was I was experiencing. I cannot account for this certainty, I only know I was sure.[4]

Rather than a Divine intervention, Doris Grumbach experienced a Divine awakening. An intervention is temporary. An awakening has staying power.

We think our deepest fear in life is that things won't turn out right. But really, our deepest fear is that when it turns out we will be alone. Once we know we're not alone, ever, there is no need of intervention because there is nothing left to fear.

---

[1] The mysterious mentor Mulla Nasrudin had hundreds of wise stories and sayings that were full of charm, wit and backhanded humour. His stories appear in literature and in oral traditions from the Middle East to Greece, Russia, France and China. Many nations claim Nasrudin as a native son. The Turks exhibit a grave showing his date of death as 386. But nobody really knows who he was or where he came from.

[2] Acts 17:28a

[3] Rabbi Abraham Joshua Heschel was considered by many to be one of the most significant Jewish theologians of the 20th century. Heschel was also known as an activitst for civil rights in the United States and an activist for freedom for Soviet Jewry. He was one of the few Jewish theologians widely read by Christians. His most influential works include *Man Is Not Alone*, *God in Search of Man*, *The Sabbath*, and *The Prophets*.

[4] Doris Grumbach, *The Presence of Absence: On Prayers and an Epiphany* (Beacon Press, 1998)

6

The Greening of God

One unusually cold April day I shivered out my back door to the parking lot. One of my neighbours was there, unlocking his car door. I yelled to him, "Hey Ivan, so much for global warming!"

He spun around, emphatically shook his finger at me and scolded, "This unseasonably cold weather is also a result of global warming, Bob."

"Do you mean it is getting colder because it is getting warmer?" I said this just to get his goat, and his goat I got.

Clearly irritated by my display of ignorance he replied, "Bob, global warming causes temperature extremes, it makes the weather weird."

To my friend and neighbour, climate change is nothing to joke about.

Climate change is indeed an inconvenient truth and more. To listen to the prognosticators, we have gone beyond inconvenient. They tell us that global warming portends the end of the world as we know it.

As Chair of the Parliament of the World's Religions, I attended a summit of the world's religious leaders at the United Nations in August of 2000. During one of the meetings, three representatives from the Inuit tribes living in the northernmost reaches of Alaska told the delegates, "Our people have lived near the polar ice cap for thousands of years. After many thousands of years we must tell you we are deeply concerned. Where our parents once stood on ice is now water. Everywhere we look the polar ice cap is melting." A great gasp spread across the UN Assembly Hall. This sounded like serious news. But it wasn't altogether clear what we could do about it. I remember thinking that surely someone else would take care of the problem. I didn't want to take it on myself.

Practically everything we are hearing about global warming indicates that an imminent environmental crisis of biblical proportion looms. If we fail to act quickly and decisively, we will be facing a doomsday scenario.

In light of the magnitude of this crisis it would be easy to take a grim perspective. But fortunately, this is not what's happening. Locally and globally, people are taking initiative and inspiring others to live a greener life.

The things we depend on, such as water, fossil fuels, air, and food, come in to us from the world out there. Conversely, the consequences of the way we use these things ripple out and affect not only our immediate surroundings but the entire global community. We share an inextricable and complex interdependence. We are irrevocably connected to the whole world. Every personal choice carries a global consequence. This gives us power. And when we act together in an intelligent and coordinated fashion, our power grows exponentially. Understanding the power we have and acting out of our empowerment is the first step to dealing with global warming.

In the 1980s, Joseph Campbell awakened public consciousness to the power of myth. A PBS interview with Bill Moyers contains the following exchange.

Moyers: Of course, we moderns are stripping the world of its natural revelations, of nature itself. I think of that pygmy legend of the little boy who finds the bird with the beautiful song in the forest and brings it home.

Campbell: He asks his father to bring food for the bird, and the father doesn't want to feed a mere bird, so he kills it. And the legend says the man killed the bird, and with the bird he killed the song, and with the song, himself. He dropped dead, completely dead, and was dead forever.

Moyers: Isn't that a story about what happens when human beings destroy their environment? Destroy their world? Destroy nature and the revelations of nature?

Campbell: They destroy their own nature, too. They kill the song.

Moyers: And isn't mythology the story of the song?

Campbell: Mythology is the song. It's the song of the imagination inspired by the energies of the body. Once a Zen master stood up before his students and was about to deliver a sermon. And just as he was about to open his mouth, a bird sang. And he said, "The sermon has been delivered."

Moyers: I was about to say that we are creating new myths, but you say no, every myth we tell today has some point of origin in our past experience.

Campbell: The main motifs of the myths are the same, and they have always been the same. If you want to find your own mythology, the key is with what society do you associate? Every mythology has grown up in a certain society and in a bounded field.[1]

The myths we carry are songs we sing about the life we share. And the songs we sing can keep us from a deep understanding and embracing of interdependency if we let them.

In the book of Genesis there are two creation myths. The story of Adam and Eve in the Garden of Eden is the second one. The first creation narrative, found in the first chapter of Genesis, begins with these words: "In the beginning God created the heavens and the earth. The earth was without form and void, and darkness was on the face of the deep; and the Spirit of God moved over the waters."

The Genesis creation narrative came into being around 600 BCE, when the Israelites were in exile in Babylon. While being held in captivity, they were exposed to the Babylonian creation myth about the young god Marduk and the older goddess Tiamet, who were involved in a cosmic battle.

During the battle, when Tiamet opened her mouth to devour Marduk, he drove in the evil wind in order that she should not be able to close her lips. Her belly became distended and she opened wide her mouth. Marduk shot off an arrow, which cut through her inward parts and split Tiamet's heart. He cast down her carcass and stood upon it.

In this Babylonian myth, Tiamet's carcass is cut asunder and the corpse of the goddess becomes the earth and the firmament of the existing world.[2]

When the Israelites were finally free of Babylonian oppression, there is evidence that they believed that the dead goddess was still underfoot. The story from Genesis says that the Spirit of God moved over "the face of the deep." In Genesis, the word for "the face of the deep" is *tehom*, which is derived from the Babylonian word Tiamet.[3]

The firmament, the earth, and the sea are reminiscent of the dead body of the Goddess. Here is a not so subtle implication that Mother Earth is dead.

Later on in Genesis God says, "Let us make human beings in our own image, after our likeness, and let them have dominion over all the earth...be fruitful and multiply and fill the earth and subdue it." We have mostly taken this to mean that God is the Spirit that moves over the dead earth. The earth is compost and the spirit of the Divine is a separate entity that uses the decay to create life. This hints at the origin of our current belief that we are somehow separate from the earth and from each other, and speaks to the reasons for the strength and depth of this belief.

In one way this story is a hopeful one. The Spirit creates life from death. However, it also implies that God is separate from the earth. It intimates that God subdues and dominates the earth. It suggests that human beings are created in the image of the Divine and are therefore separate from the earth, with the right to subdue and dominate it. Ancient myths have a way of lodging deeply in the collective psyche and providing subtle rationale for treating the earth as an object to be dominated and exploited. As such, this story/myth contains the root of the beliefs that allow us to propagate and propitiate the behaviours that feed our current ecological crisis.

Thankfully, we are beginning to wake up and see the earth with new eyes. We are waking up because our experience of the life we share on this earth is changing. Other unfamiliar ancient myths are being discovered and re-created in new forms, such as the Gaia hypothesis, which was developed nearly 30 years ago by British scientist James Lovelock. Lovelock suggested that the biosphere is not a machine with many parts, but rather a living organism with one mind. Lovelock says that things such as the regulation of salt in the seas and oxygen in the air can only be explained if we consider the earth to be a single living organism.[4]

When the Gaia hypothesis was presented it sounded like a new and radical idea. But it is not new at all. Indigenous cultures have always celebrated the universe as a living organism. She has been known variously as Mother Earth, the Great Mother, the Goddess. Today's indigenous peoples represent a continuous embodiment of the most ancient spiritual wisdom on the earth. This wisdom teaches that everything in the universe is born out of something else. Every human has a mother. Everybody has a father. But every life materializes from the body of Mother Earth.

For the last three thousand years or so, the metaphor of the Divine feminine has been suppressed. When speaking of the Divine in a sermon, I occasionally use the word *goddess*. Invariably, someone approaches me after and says that the word *goddess* goes just a little too far for them. Many of these same people can live with the metaphor of God as father, but having a feminine God, a Goddess, is incomprehensible.

Ingrained in our collective unconscious is a patriarchal world view. It may be true enough that the concepts of male supremacy and male dominance are eschewed in many countries, but the impression of patriarchy lingers in the collective consciousness. Literally, patriarchy means that men hold the power in society, which includes having power over women. Throughout history, this notion of patriarchy has been adopted and absorbed by both sexes and then expressed in myriad ways, one of which is a discomfort with Goddess.

At the heart of the patriarchal value system is the conviction that is morally justifiable for some of us to dominate others of us. The patriarchal system also permits violence as a means to preserve the balance of power. The key idea of patriarchy is "the right to dominate." It has taken thousands of years but we have just about completed our domination of the body of the earth. We have also tasted the bitter fruit of humans seeking domination over other humans. And hopefully we have learned that domination creates suffering not only for the dominated but also the dominator.

The feminine, the Goddess, knows nothing of domination. Any apparent "destruction" is for the purpose of regeneration, not control or obliteration. The intention is to begin anew, not to oppress. The aim is to enable a new beginning, not create a final ending. The heat of the forest fire may kill the trees but it allows many seeds to germinate that otherwise would not. Autumn, to winter, to spring.

When we acknowledge the Goddess as Creator, we see the whole universe as her body. All life emerges from her body.

And because everything emerges from the same source, life is something to be shared.

In seeking a greener, friendlier image of God, many religious people talk about becoming better stewards of the earth. This is clearly a healthier impulse. To practise stewardship is to take care of the resources that belong to somebody else. To practise stewardship is to use our resources in a responsible way. When people talk about the stewardship of the earth, what they typically mean is that we must take care of the earth for future generations.

However, I am not one to use the word *stewardship*, especially when speaking of our responsibility to the earth. Stewardship means well. It doesn't seek to dominate or subdue anyone or anything. But stewardship implies that God is distant, that God is away, that God is somehow beyond, above, or outside the earth.

It is my experience is that the Divine is right here with us, winking, nodding and waving all the time. She is present and voluptuous and she wants to dance with us.

Fredrick Buechner describes an ordinary drive he took one summer:

Suddenly, I started noticing the trees.

They were in full summer foliage. They were greener than I think I have ever seen trees before. The sun was in them. The air was stirring them. They rose noble and plumed against the sky. The branches were heavy with leaves. As I drove by, they waved at me. They beckoned. They reached out. It was the wind, of course, that made them wave. It was the air whipped up by my car streaking by at 65 miles per hour. But no matter. They waved in the only way trees have of waving and caught my attention so completely that all other thoughts vanished from my head, including my thoughts about them. I didn't think about them. I just saw them. I didn't put words to what was happening. I just let it happen. I just happened with it. It was a rare and precious drive for as much longer as it lasted, and it was only when I got where I was going that I found myself putting words to it at last.

The trees are always so glad to see us – those were the words I put to it. I'd never noticed that before. They waved their branches like flags in a parade, hailing me as I passed by as though I were some mighty spirit. They looked as if they had lined up for miles along the New York Thruway to greet me, and, at the risk of seeming hopelessly eccentric, I confess that, after a while, I found myself waving back at them every once in a while, as if they too, were mighty spirits and I was greeting them. At the risk of seeming even more eccentric still, I believe that this was not just a fantasy of mine. I believe that for a little while I saw those trees as so real that I was myself made real by them. It was the whole of me that waved to the whole of them...what it was that we were hailing and honoring in each other – was that it was Almighty God who had formed and given life to us both, that trees and humans together bear within them as the indivisible wholeness and holiness...The trees waved their holy branches at my holiness. I waved my holy hand at theirs.[5]

Divine Presence is always within us and around us. The Holy One is always winking, nodding, and waving to us. Divine Presence is there when we go to work or gather with family and friends. Divine Presence is there when we gaze out upon a sunset or up at the stars at night. Each and every life, and all of life pulsates with Divine energy. When I am open to it I see it. I experience it. I know that I am in it and it is in me.

To believe the Divine is in everything and everything in it is called *panentheism*. This should not be confused with pantheism. Pantheism says that God is *in* everything. Panentheism says that not only is God in everything, everything is also in God – which means that where there is life, there is God. God is not the dominator; rather, God is the connector. Everywhere we go we find the Sacred, because God is life itself. Everything lives in the Holy Presence, and God in everything that lives.

Water and air pollution, deforestation, and global warming are all symptoms of a deep brokenness. And of course we must address these symptoms of our global ecological crisis.

But the real crisis is relational. And the more we commit ourselves to living *with* the earth, the greener God becomes.

[1]   Joseph Campbell with Bill Moyers, *The Power of Myth* (Anchor Books, 1988)
[2]   Walter Wink, *The Powers That Be* (Galilee 1998)
[3]   Gottwald, Norman, *A Light to the Nations* (Harper and Row, 1959)
[4]   James Lovelock, *Gaia: A New Look at Life on Earth* (Oxford Univeristy Press, 1979, Third Edition 2000)
[5]   Frederick Buechner, *Theology Today*, January 1993, vol. 49, no. 4

PART II

Be a Christ

... ❦ ...

When the Christian tradition represents Jesus' death as foreordained by God, as necessary to the divine plan for salvation, and as obediently accepted by Jesus the Son out of love for God the Father, God is made into a child abuser or a bystander to violence against his own child.

~ Rita Nakashima Brock, *Proverbs of Ashes: Redemptive Suffering and the Search for What Saves Us* (Beacon Press, 2001)

The living Christ is the Christ of Love who is always generating love, moment after moment. When the church manifests understanding, tolerance and loving-kindness, Jesus is there. Christians have to help Jesus Christ be manifested by their way of life, showing those around them that love, understanding, and tolerance are possible.

~ Thich Nhat Hanh

7

What Christians Have Done to Jesus

In 1973 I was in my last quarter in seminary. The time had come for me to face the ordination council of the American Baptist Churches of the West. Candidates had been instructed to answer 25 questions on matters ranging from the meaning of ministry to those more explicitly theological. I completed my paper and handed it over to my faculty advisor who commented, "Well, nobody else has written this much."

Chuckling, he added, "It's all the more rope to hang you with." Then he grinned and said, "Naw, I'm only kidding."

Kidding or not, it turned out he was right.

I walked into the boardroom and faced 14 dour men dressed in suits and ties. It was obvious my sports jacket, ponytail and bell-bottom jeans were not going to win any fashion awards from this group.

I soon discovered that every other comment of mine became fodder for the next round of disagreements for that group of largely conservative pastors. The interview seemed interminable. Finally, it came time for me to leave the room. I waited in the lobby for what seemed like an eternity before learning the results of their vote: seven *yes*, six *no*, and one abstention. By the skin of my teeth I qualified for ordination.

As I walked out of the building with my faculty advisor, he took out his handkerchief and wiped his brow. I turned to him and said, "Bill, I thought all these people had a theological education."

He replied, "It doesn't have anything to do with a theological education. It has to do with what makes you feel secure." In a very mentor-like fashion he added, "I want you to read a sermon by Harry Emerson Fosdick. It's called *What Christians have done to Christ*."

Several years later I read the Fosdick sermon. In it, Fosdick says, "Christians have dressed Jesus up in the scarlet robe of metaphysical concepts of Deity; they have pushed him off as in the Byzantine frescoes, into a distant heaven, until Christ, the real Christ who grew up in Nazareth, who taught beside the lake, who challenged the bigotry of priests, refused to bend before the power of Rome, prayed in an agony of need in the garden, and died courageously on Calvary, has been covered up in theological silks and satins. It is not his enemies who have done to him this dreadful thing; it is his friends."[1]

Mainstream scholars have reached a consensus that a definitive portrait of the historical Jesus cannot be painted and that an uncovered Jesus looks more like an unfinished sketch. So how did we come to dress up Jesus in these theological silks and satins?

The Mediterranean Jewish rabbi named Jesus taught with stories, parables and crisp sayings. He evidently spoke with incredible clarity and amazing simplicity. When he preached, performed a miracle, or gave a teaching, he talked about the kingdom of God. He said that the kingdom of God is around us, that we are in it, and that it is in us. He did not mention the kingdom of Jesus.

A movement swirled about this magnetic rabbi. Jesus walked his talk. The oppressed, the marginalized, and the outcasts were drawn to him by the promise that the power of God belonged to them in the here and now.

The religious and political authorities felt threatened and conspired to end the movement by crucifying Jesus. They succeeded in the latter but could not suppress the movement, as reports of the Resurrection grew and the nascent movement gained momentum. House churches were formed. Diverse in their beliefs, these early Christian communities welcomed newcomers. The new movement was particularly attractive to the early followers because they lived in a world of hardship and suffering, and there was great comfort in the thought that their daily crucifixions could be overcome.

The heterogeneous movement continued to grow. The pagan emperor Constantine reportedly had a vision of Christ in the year 312 and this led to his own conversion. Constantine eventually declared Christianity the religion of the empire. What had begun as a movement became an institution.

Perhaps the defining moment for Christian orthodoxy occurred in 325 when the bishops gathered to quash, once and for all, the lure of heresy. They gathered in Nicea (in what is now Turkey) and thrashed out and adopted the Nicene creed, which expresses the view that Jesus is essentially no different from God the Father. Thus it became official doctrine that God and Jesus are of one and the same substance. Only pagans and heretics could believe otherwise. The authority of the bishops had become the definition of truth.[2]

Those in power (then and now) sought to protect their authority by creating social and religious conventions that silenced dissenters and the marginalized, and favoured those in power. And, overwhelmingly, we still take the bait and believe there is only one way to be a Christian. We have been seduced into assuming that being a Christian has to do with believing in Jesus in the ways proscribed by others, who have in turn received their ideas from others, who have themselves received their ideas from others, and so on.

Christians have put Christ under glass. Jesus has been separated from us. In order to worship him we have covered him in the robes of saviour of the known universe. Here is a Jesus dressed as a king, even though he refused to say he was one. Here is Jesus sanctified as intercessor when he consistently taught that the realm of God is already within us and in our midst.

Seventy years ago Harry Emerson Fosdick said, "(Christians) get rid of Jesus by adoring him, by making him God, by pushing him off to some distant heaven, by thinking of him mainly over the high altar of the church, safely distant from their daily lives, by putting him into magnificent creeds the words of which Jesus himself would not know the meaning...[3]

Jesus violated the social and religious conventions of the time in order to bear witness to the realm of God. Jesus showed us what heaven on earth is like. He surrounded himself with the poor, the maimed, and every other manner of outcast. And so those in power considered him to be a threat to their authority. Religious leaders were always trying to make him look bad in order to de-legitimize his message. The real teachings were cross-dressed in order to mislead – that way, the power of the leaders would not be threatened.

There was once a doctor who was summoned to a household by the wife of a man lying stricken in his bed. As soon as the doctor arrived at the house, the woman took him to examine the motionless figure in the bed. After a few moments of examining the man, the doctor turned and said to the woman, "I am sorry to say that your husband is no more, my dear."

But a feeble sound of protest came from the unmoving figure in the bed. "No, I'm still alive!"

"Hold your tongue!" snapped the woman. "The doctor knows better than you."

"Hold your tongue" is what the authorities said to Jesus. And "hold your tongue" is what the church has said to non-believers and Christian heretics for nearly two millennia.

Jesus refused to hold his tongue.

When asked what the greatest commandment was, Jesus said, "You shall love the Lord your God with all your heart, soul and mind. And the second is like the first. You shall love your neighbour as yourself. On these two commandments depends all the law and the prophets."[4]

The greatest commandment is to love God. The second greatest is to love your neighbour as yourself. Nowhere does Jesus say the greatest commandment is to believe that he is the one and only, the Son of God. He does not say there is only one way to God, and he's it. Jesus doesn't reduce the mystery of life to the dogma of belief.

As William Sloane Coffin said, "Too many religious people make faith their aim. They think 'the greatest of these' is faith and that faith defined as all but infallible doctrine. These are the dogmatic, divisive Christians, more concerned with freezing the doctrine than warming the heart. If faith can be exclusive, love can only be inclusive."[5]

When Jesus is undressed, when the "theological silks and satins" are removed, when Jesus is unveiled, what do we see?

We see that real religion has nothing to do with what we say we believe. Real religion has to do with how we actually live our lives. Jesus' vision of the Kingdom of God proclaimed a radical program of non-violent resistance to all forms of religious, political and social domination. Jesus tells us to let our spirits resist oppression by living out of our resilience. He challenges us to take the difficult path and not be led astray by our egoic selves.

We get a hint of this program in the *Sermon on the Mount* where he teaches that we should love the people we love to hate. If we are in conflict with somebody, we should find a way to reconcile. If someone wrongs us seventy-seven times, we must forgive that person not only once, but seventy-seven times. And when we throw a party, we should invite the poor, the maimed, the lame and the blind. The first people to invite to our fancy party are those who cannot possibly repay us. If we get slapped on the right cheek, we should turn the other cheek. By returning hatred for hatred, or violence for violence, we are hating and doing violence to ourselves

Do unto others as you would have them do unto you.

The unveiled Jesus reveals to us that belief and religion are not enough. What you do is what you really and truly believe.

The unveiled Jesus asks us tough questions. Who do we think we are? What does our life serve? How do we treat others? How are we living our lives here and now?

Jesus asks us how big our circle of compassion is. Who are we leaving out? Whoever it is, bring them in.

Jesus is the question, not the answer. This is Jesus unveiled.

[1] Harry Emerson Fosdick, *Successful Christian Living* (Harper and Brothers, 1937)
[2] Elaine Pagels, *Beyond Belief* (Random House, 2003) 168–174
[3] Harry Emerson Fosdick, *Successful Christian Living* (Harper and Brothers, 1973)
[4] Mark 12:28-31
[5] William Sloane Coffin, *Credo* (Westminster John Knox Press, 2004)

8

We Are Transmitters

... ༄༅༅ ...

At the age of ten, I climbed aboard a church bus on my way to a Billy Graham Crusade in San Francisco. The members of our group of about 30 adults and a handful of children were full of holy excitement and sanctified anticipation and we pumped ourselves up by singing gospel songs with great gusto all the way.

We finally arrived in the parking lot of the huge auditorium known as Cow Palace, where a sea of parked cars and buses stretched before us. The very sight of such a crowd served as a confirmation to my ten-year-old eyes that something momentous was about to occur.

Inside the Palace, after struggling through the crowded lobby and climbing the stairs to my seat, I stepped out onto the upper deck and saw a vast, elliptical auditorium filled to capacity. The place was buzzing with expectant energy. The Crusade Choir had assembled on the platform in front of the big, bright blue banner proclaiming, "I am the way, the truth, the life." Crusade choir director Cliff Barrows raised his arms and several hundred voices sang out. Billy Graham delivered his sermon with his typical winsome presence and compelling words.

Then, at the dramatic climax of the service, the choir and audience sang together and I knew it was my time to take the walk.

Pulled up out of my chair by the tug of the Spirit, heart pounding, I was carried by the singing throng to the platform where Billy Graham stood. In the presence of 15,000 witnesses, I publicly declared that I believed in Jesus Christ as my personal lord and saviour.

Following the service, I met with one of the Crusade counsellors. He told me that because I had accepted Jesus Christ as my personal lord and saviour, everything in my life would be taken care of. I would know real peace because I now knew Jesus. And most importantly, when I died I would claim heaven as my prize.

It was heady stuff.

But after only a few days, the glow of that night faded. The newness wore off, and I realized my life was proceeding pretty much as it always had. I still had problems, fears, and doubts. Worse yet, I was still overweight. Over the next few years, as life went on without much change, the light of my evangelical exuberance waned.

Nevertheless, I have discovered that something from that evening has remained a part of me, even though I have outgrown the initial zeal. In recent years, I have realized that the one thing about the Christian tradition that is inextricably woven into my spiritual DNA is Jesus. But now I know a different Jesus than the one I met at the Billy Graham Crusade.

Many people worship Jesus. For the vast majority of Christians, Jesus is the whole message. According to conventional Christianity, Jesus is God in human form, the lamb of God who takes away the sins of the world.

I know what it means to believe in Jesus as personal lord and saviour, but that kind of believing no longer makes sense to me. To believe that the historical figure of Jesus is a divine redeemer seems like a wish, a fantasy. It has nothing to do with life as I have experienced it.

If the Jesus of history were to materialize before us today, and we were to ask him to condense his message into one sentence, I think that, like Mahatma Gandhi he would say that his life is his message.

And Jesus might also point out that this is how it is for us too. How we think, how we act, how we treat others, and how we live our lives in general is the message we are giving to ourselves and to the world.

This is why I now believe *with* Jesus, rather than *in* Jesus.

I believe with Jesus that by learning to love our enemies we learn the true meaning of love. I believe with Jesus that the light of the Holy Presence is in everyone. I believe with Jesus that the kingdom of God is within us and among us. I believe with Jesus that the Divine looks after us, like the lilies of the field, whether we know it or not.

Jesus teaches that spiritual truth is a process, not a product. This differs from seeing religious truth as a fixed body of beliefs, a commodity that we can buy into.

There is the story in the gospels about a wealthy young man who asked Jesus how he could find eternal life.[1] This young man knew that he was a child of privilege. His possessions and social position satisfied his surface needs, but deep down he felt empty. He asked Jesus what he could do to fill the gaping hole inside him and how he could be assured of eternal life.

Jesus said to him, "Follow the commandments. You must love God with all your heart, soul, and mind and you must love your neighbour as yourself. Do these things and you will have eternal life."

But the wealthy young man quickly responded, "This is what I have been doing, but something is still missing from my life."

Jesus paused, then answered, "Well then, there is one more thing you can do. Sell everything you have, then give your money to the poor, and follow me."

This was the one thing the young man could not do. He was too attached to his prestige and wealth to be able to give them up.

The young man had come to Jesus looking for something concrete, like a definitive answer, a product or an outcome. Jesus offered him a process instead.

Jesus said, "You come to me for a message, but I am telling you that your life is the message."

D. H. Lawrence wrote, "As we live we are transmitters of life, and when we fail to transmit life, life fails to flow through us...Give and it shall be given unto you is still the truth about life...But giving life is not so easy...It means kindling the life quality where it was not."[2]

The wealthy young man wanted only to receive, but Jesus told him that he could not receive what he really wanted unless he was able to give. Jesus told him that he could not live a life of real

importance unless he was willing to let go of his self-import.
He would always feel as though he was missing something as
long as he held on to his ego, his sense of separate self.

The Buddhist teacher Pema Chodron compares living in the
ego to living in a room.

> Ego is like a room of your own, a room with a view, with
> the temperature and the smells that you like the most.
> You want it your own way. You'd just like to have a little
> peace; you'd like to have a little happiness, you know, just
> 'Gimme a break!'
>
> The more you try to get life to come out so that it will
> always suit you, the more your fear of other people and
> what's outside the room grows. Rather than becoming
> more relaxed, you start pulling down the shades and
> locking the door. When you do go out, you find the
> experience unsettling and disagreeable. You become
> touchier, more fearful, more irritable than ever. The
> more you just try to get it your way, the less you feel at
> home.
>
> To begin to develop compassion for yourself and
> others, you have to unlock the door. At first, you don't
> open it yet because you have to work with your fear that
> somebody you don't like might come in. Then as you
> begin to relax and befriend those feelings, you begin to
> open it. Sure enough, in come the music and the smells
> that we don't like. Sure enough, someone puts a foot in
> and tells you that you should be of a different religion or
> vote for someone you don't like or give money that you
> don't want to give.

When you begin to face the feelings, you become curious as to why you respond that way. You develop some compassion, connecting with your inner self. You relate with what begins to happen when you aren't protecting yourself so much. Then gradually you become more curious than afraid. To be fearless isn't really to overcome fear, it's to come to know its nature. Just open the door and at some point you'll feel capable of inviting all sentient beings as your guests.[3]

We all know what it is like to be holed up in the small room of the ego. When we open up and begin to transmit life, we air out the little mind that keeps the heart closed.

To do this requires courage and the willingness to face ourselves and our fears every day. To take this journey requires the discipline of practices like prayer and meditation and the support of a spiritual community. Living this way, in openness, compassion, and loving kindness, we wake up to see our connections to others, even the people who frightened us.

The miracle of miracles is that we realize there is really only one life that is being lived in the world through each and every one of us. To see we are all living one life is the heart of the message of Jesus, and the truth of transmitting life.

So this is life. Life is going to bed every night, getting up in the morning, going to school, going to work, sitting down to eat, doing the dishes. Life is wonderful connection, painful disconnection, loss and profound grief. Life is hundreds of thousands of fearful, funny, and joyous moments. What else were we expecting?

Each moment is a lifetime in and of itself. We remember the past and plan for the future. And wherever we go there we are.

We live in an eternal now. This is it. This is life as it really is. Spiritual truth is not about being transported to a different kind of life. It is about fully living the moment we are in.

There is no product, religion, or relationship that will tie up all our loose ends and open the gates of paradise, nirvana, or heaven for us. Yet here and there we catch our breath, the soul is refreshed, the heart is opened. When the heart is opened, our lives become a feast of delight.

Jesus taught that the spiritual truth for living and breathing human beings is a lifetime journey. And along our way we try to remember to forget ourselves and be the message.

Waking up to the spiritual life we find the Divine within ourselves. And when this happens, we see it in everyone. To see this one Holy Presence in all puts everything in perspective. We learn to take spiritual sustenance from knowing that God is in everyone and everything. We learn to see that life is a great banquet of the Divine and that there is a place at this table for each and every one of us.

Frederick Buechner writes:

> God is the comic shepherd who gets more of a kick out of that one lost sheep once God finds it again than out of the ninety and nine who had the good sense not to get lost in the first place. God is the eccentric host who goes out into the skid rows and soup kitchens and charity wards and brings home a freak show for dinner. God brings home the man with no legs who sells shoelaces at the corner. There's the woman in the moth-eaten fur coat who makes her daily rounds of the garbage cans. There's the old wino with his pint in a brown paper

bag, the drug dealer, the prostitute. And then there's the village idiot who stands at the blinker light waving his hand as the cars go by. They are all seated at the damask-laid table in the great hall. The candles are all lit and the champagne glasses filled. At a sign from the host, the musicians strike up *Amazing Grace*. If you have to explain it, don't bother.[4]

Living the spiritual truth is to wake up to the banquet of life in whatever way it is dished out to us in the here and now. It is to know intuitively that we are all part of one another and of a larger whole. From the beasts of the field to the poor in Calcutta, from those who walk the corridors of power to those who languish powerlessly on their deathbeds, we are all a part of each other. And it is only as the heart is stirred by this truth that we begin to wake up to our true spiritual nature. We wake up and live our lives as the message. We transmit life.

There is a story of an ancient Indian teacher who gathered her students together and said, "Today I am going to test the level of your spiritual awareness."

She pointed to some chickens that were running around and said, "I want each of you to take a chicken and an axe. You are to kill these chickens with your axe. There is only one condition. You must be certain that no one can see you. I don't want anyone to see what you are doing."

The students went out to complete their task.

The next day two of the three students returned. One told of climbing a rocky mountain, struggling to get to the top as the chicken fought to escape. When he arrived and was certain that the only thing around him was blue sky, he killed the chicken.

The other told of finding a cave and going deep into the darkness, where he took the axe to the neck of the chicken and killed it. He was positive no one had seen him.

As the second student finished telling his story, the third student appeared on the horizon. As he got closer, it became apparent that he was still carrying his chicken, and it was very much alive.

The other two students smirked arrogantly. The teacher smiled and asked, "Well, what have we here?"

The third student answered, "I found the perfect spot. It was completely isolated. But every time I raised my axe, I looked into the chicken's eyes and realized it was impossible to do this without someone watching."

With this the teacher said, "You, my child, have passed the test.

"The Divine spark is in a chicken. It is in everything."

A story like this is a metaphor for seeing ourselves in all of life and seeing all of life in us. Whatever I do to another, I do to myself. Whatever I do to myself, I do to another.

We all live our many lives, but really we are living one life – together.

There's nobody here but us chickens.

[1] Mark 10:17–22
[2] D. H. Lawrence, *We Are Transmitters* (Poemhunter.com)
[3] Pema Chodron, *Start Where You Are* (Shambhala, 1994)
[4] Frederick Buechner, *Telling the Truth: Gospel as Tragedy, Comedy and Fairy Tale* (HarperSanFrancisco, 1977)

9

The Cross Is Dressed in
Interpretative Drag

••• ❧ •••

In my high school senior yearbook, there is a picture of me dressed in drag. It was taken after a talent show or stage production, I can't remember which. I do recall wearing a tight red dress. As a varsity football player and serious jock, I took great pleasure in how people were shocked by my short dress, silk stockings and long blonde wig. My friends said I was a knockout.

Transvestites cross-dress for many different reasons. Some do it for fun. Others do it because their true sexual identity does not match the body they were born in. Whatever the reason, to cross-dress is to masquerade, to impersonate, to present an image that belies what is underneath it.

Although he doesn't mention cross-dressing as such, Jesus scholar Robert Funk says we need to look at Jesus with new eyes.

Jesus, he says, has been cast in the myth of the external redeemer and hero. This myth says the world is fatally flawed and can be redeemed only from without.[1] In the external redeemer myth, the hero comes from beyond. Although cloaked in human guise, the external redeemer is not one of us.

The traditional interpretation of the crucifixion story parallels the external redeemer myth. The official doctrine of the Christian church (Protestant, Catholic, and Orthodox) has clothed Jesus in the dress of benevolent god/man. The Jesus of conventional Christianity is dressed in the interpretive drag of this external redeemer.

In conventional Christianity, the central meaning of the cross is atonement by blood. Jesus had to die on the cross so that when we die we will have "eternal life."

As Marcus Borg says, it can be hard to believe this.

> The notion that God's only son came to this planet to offer his life as a sacrifice for the sins of the world, and that we are saved by believing this story, is simply incredible. Taken metaphorically, this story can be very powerful. But taken literally, it is a profound obstacle to accepting the Christian message. Too many people, it simply makes no sense, and I think we need to be straightforward about that.[2]

Conventional doctrine teaches that Jesus took on all the sins of the world when he was crucified. We have been taught that Jesus had to die on the cross so that when we die we will have eternal life. Jesus was the lamb of God and the human sacrifice necessary to remove the blot of original sin on the human soul. However, in the gospels, Jesus is never quoted as saying that he came to take away the sins of the world by death on the cross. It was other New Testament writers who interpreted the cross in this way and said that Jesus was the lamb of God who came to take away the sins of the world. This is the cross in interpretive drag.

Many scholars agree that this idea can be traced to the ancient practices of nomadic Hebrews who sacrificed animals in order to appease God. In the Old Testament book of Leviticus, strict instructions are given around the requirement of making an animal sacrifice for the forgiveness of sin. In Chapter 4, we read,

> If he brings a lamb as an offering for a sin offering, a female lamb without blemish shall be brought. He shall lay his hand upon it and kill it...then the priest shall take some of the blood of the sin offering with his finger and put it in the horns of the altar of burnt offering, and pour out the rest of its blood at the base of the altar. And all of its fat he shall remove as a peace offering, and the priest shall burn it on the altar and make an atonement for the sin he has committed and he shall be forgiven.[3]

The lamb, the livestock, was given as a peace offering to God.

There was also another ritual practised by the ancient Hebrews. On the Day of Atonement, the high priest would take a goat, symbolically cover it with the sins of all the people, and send it out into the wilderness. Bearing everyone's blame and being forced to suffer on everyone's behalf, the innocent goat became a scapegoat.

Out of this theological perspective and cultural context, many New Testament writers then proclaimed the cross to be the definitive blood sacrifice. Jesus was like a pure and innocent lamb, a peace offering unto God. Jesus became our scapegoat, taking the consequences for our sin so that we wouldn't have to take it on ourselves.

Add to this the prevailing notion at the time that God was separate, vengeful, and willing to forgive only when there was retribution, pain and the shedding of blood and we have the cross in interpretive drag. One thing became another.

After hearing a summary of conventional Christian theology, D. T. Suzuki, one of the great Zen teachers of the 20th century, said, "Ah, so it is God against man and man against nature. A very strange religion."

We have been taught to look at the cross through the eyes of the unredeemed. We are told that when Jesus died on the cross, he did something for us that we can't do for ourselves. He bore and carried away all our sins, the sins of the world.

I was taught this interpretation of the cross as I was growing up and I had a childhood image of Jesus being weighed down by all these sins being heaped upon him. I had a mental picture of the cross piled high with every ignominious thought, word and deed, every great pain and torment that ever was and would be.

I was also taught that since Jesus was above it all, an external redeemer, he could handle it. Since he was fully divine, he was superhuman. He was playing a role, acting out his part and it was all God's plan.

In Central and South America, the cross is often a symbol of liberation from oppression. For many, the cross is an icon which helps them not to feel alone in their suffering. The Celtic cross is characterized by a circle at the cross beams symbolizing the union of opposites: circles and lines, female and male. Some say the Celtic cross originated in the *kiakra* of Vedic mythology, a sign of sexual union.

Whatever the case, the cross is a powerful symbol. And it carries a lot of baggage.

I have many Jewish friends who tell me they recoil upon seeing a cross prominently displayed in a Christian church. Jewish congregations that use Christian sanctuaries for the celebration of high holy days typically cover or remove the cross from the sanctuary during their observances. For many years, my rabbi friends refused invitations to participate in our annual interfaith service. It came as a surprise to me when one of them finally told me, "I know when you offer Communion to everyone you are doing it in a sensitive and inclusive way. But as a Jew I can't do Communion. Too much baggage."

The cross is a powerful symbol.

There is another myth. Joseph Campbell speaks of the hero with a thousand faces. This hero is born in and of this world, leaves home, undergoes trials and tribulations, overcomes evil and obstacles of every kind, and finally returns home to bestow blessings on others. The hero with a thousand faces redeems the world from within.

If Jesus were able to speak to us today about that death on a cross, what might he say to us? What might he say about what its meaning?

Jesus never talks about his death being sacrificial. What mattered most to him was relationship – relationship with God, with family, with friends, with each other. In the four canonical gospels Jesus speaks seven times from the cross. One time he talks about being thirsty, another time he says, "It is finished." His life and his ministry are fulfilled. The other five times have to do with his relationships. One gospel narrative tells of some women, perhaps close friends, standing by the side of the road as Jesus struggled with the load of the cross. They wept as Jesus struggled. They saw the injustice of it all, the suffering and imminent death that lay ahead. They identified with him. On hearing their weeping, Jesus stopped. With dry, parched lips he formed the words, "Daughters of Jerusalem, don't weep for me."

But still they cried out.

Again Jesus insists, "Don't weep for me, weep for yourselves and for your children."

Do not weep for only one, weep for everyone.

Relationships.

Jesus reminds us that we are related to him in our predictable and even our senseless crucifixions. He tells us to see our own lives reflected in the cross.

In other words, Christ suffered not to keep us from suffering but because we already suffer. Christ hung there because we already hang. Christ suffered because we already hurt, cried because we cry, died because we have to die.

The suffering of one is the suffering of all. The one cross is every cross. Every cross is reflected in one cross. It doesn't matter what colour the face. It doesn't matter what attitude or ideology someone holds. It doesn't matter how old or young, how rich or poor, whether male or female, gay, lesbian, transgendered. It just doesn't matter. The suffering of another always puts us in touch with our own suffering.

And it is by facing this suffering that we experience transformation.

According to the gospel stories, what mattered to Jesus in his dying moments is what matters to us all in our dying moments. Dying human beings care most about the people around them and about God, for whom the soul yearns. Life is stripped to the bare essentials and freed of all illusions.

We know that everyone dies, but we really don't believe it will happen to us. We know that everything is impermanent yet we live as if nothing will ever change. But when we witness a crucifixion or when we find ourselves on the crucible of existence, our illusions are peeled away.

The last illusion to go is the ego. Ego is the illusion that we who live in these differently shaped bags of flesh and bone are separate from each other, and separate from God.

Perhaps one day we visit a terminally ill friend. We enter the room and see an emaciated figure, the mere shell of the person we once knew. It is painful to look into the face of this dear one. But suddenly we meet their eyes and something happens. Locked into a momentary yet timeless gaze, there is no time or space, and no boundaries. There is the recognition that despite our separate forms, we are not separated.

Before the cross of Jesus, we discern the truth of our lives. We recognize our shared pain, suffering, and angst. And we are delivered from none of it. The cross is a timeless mirror reflecting back our fragility that is, in an odd way, a gift. From the cross of Jesus streams the light of truth.

The cross reminds us that, like Jesus, we are not destroyed by our crucifixions. We know that nothing can destroy us, no matter what happens. For even though we walk through the valley of the shadow of death, there is nothing to fear but fear itself.

And herein lays a great mystery. The cross is an emblem of death, but when we look deeply into it we see that death is not the end.

The deeper meaning of a crucifixion is that one way of life is about to be over and another is about to begin.

1   Robert W. Funk, *Honest to Jesus* (HarperSanFrancisco 1996)
2   Marcus Borg, *Meeting Jesus Again for the First Time* (HarperSanFrancisco 1994) 131
3   Leviticus 4:32–35

10

When You Sin, Grin

Many members of my congregation grew up in churches where they were taught the rationalization of original sin. As a line in the movie *The Big Chill* puts it, "Rationalizations are more important than sex. How many days have you gone without a good rationalization?"

The rationalization of the doctrine of original sin teaches that the human soul is tainted. Sin, we are told, is embedded in our spiritual DNA. Human beings are flawed.

There is empirical evidence to support this point of view. From child abductions to child abuse, from street crimes to white-collar crime, from terrorists to tyrants, from pre-emptive wars to heartless globalization, from politicians on the take to pornographers exploiting sex, it's easy to argue that human beings are sinful and cursed.

It is true that each of us carries the capacity for committing terribly destructive acts. But at the same time we have the ability to perform wonderfully compassionate deeds. It's also easy to believe that the good parts of us come from God. But where do the evil parts come from? Is there an inborn defect in human nature?

Sometime back, my wife, Judy, and I went to Japan to visit our newborn grandson. While there we developed terrible colds. When the time came to return home, I boarded the plane and sat down, holding a wad of tissues in one hand and a box of cough drops in the other. I carefully covered my mouth when coughing, and muffled my sneezes as much as possible.

Then it hit me.

On many previous occasions I had boarded a plane only to be seated near someone who was sniffling or coughing. Every time that person coughed or sneezed, I had cringed and held my breath. Whenever there was a sick person on the same plane as me, I would think, "You so and so, why did you get on this plane? Don't you have any consideration for other people? You're going to make us all sick!"

Sitting on that plane in Narita Airport it came home to me that I had become the very thing I abhorred. My self-righteous moral certitude was coming back on me. I was twice a sinner: once for indulging in unseemly behaviour, and once for my judgment of others behaving in the same way. On that return trip from Tokyo, I met the enemy, and the enemy was me.

Some would define sin as a "failure of right belief." Others would identify sin as "unseemly behaviour." Whatever the definition, calling something a sin requires a judgment. And thus, one person's sin could be another person's virtue.

In her book *Pilgrim at Tinker Creek,* Annie Dillard writes, "Somewhere, and I can't find where, I read about an Eskimo hunter who asked the local missionary priest, 'If I did not know about God and sin, would I go to hell?'

'No,' said the priest, 'not if you did not know.'

'So why did you tell me?' asked the Eskimo."[1]

Many people are surprised to learn that the definition for sin in the New Testament has nothing to do with the inherent wickedness or corruption of the human species. In the gospels, sin is literally translated to mean, "to miss the mark."

The word sin is etymologically linked to the word *sunder,* which means "to break apart." Rather than thinking of sin as a single event like the breaking of a rule, such as a traffic violation, it is more useful to see sin as a condition or state of being in which we see ourselves as literally separated from ourselves, others and the Divine.

Theologian Paul Tillich said that sin is the condition of being estranged, or seeing ourselves separated from ourselves or others.

In May of 1373, the Christian mystic Julian of Norwich received her revelations, or, as she called them, her showings. During these showings, she conversed at length with God on the topic of sin. She was told that we fall into sin not because we are wicked or corrupt, but because we are naïve. There is no stain on the soul, we are merely ignorant. We sin, that is, we are estranged from others, because we don't know any better.

Most importantly, Julian was shown that sin is not something for which we are handed out punishment. The sense of separation and the feelings of alienation are themselves the consequences.

We enter into these conditions ourselves. We suffer from within.

Inevitably we all wake up one day only to find ourselves estranged and alienated from someone, somewhere. We are estranged not because we are bad or corrupt, but because we don't know what we are doing. If someone is mean spirited, the meanness is a result of ignorance. If someone is malicious, the hatefulness is the result of not knowing any better. If we are apathetic, our indifference is a result of not knowing how to be connected and engaged to life.

Every failure in relationship to God, every failure in relationship among and between us, is a result of being ignorant to the ways of love. When we don't know how to live together it is because we don't know how to love each other, or ourselves.

Every dastardly deed, every abusive action, every greedy, self-absorbed thought, word, and deed is a result of our ignorance. Whether it is a terrorist hijacking or a mundane insensitive oversight, it stems from the same thing: our ignorance as to how to love fully and utterly. There is no list of Top Twenty sins that God doles out appropriate punishments for. There is only the failure to love.

The more we drift from love, the more we miss the mark and punish ourselves. Love is giving without expecting to receive. Love allows kindness and compassion. In the absence of love we sin, we miss the mark. We act selfishly. We close our hearts.

In *Field Notes on the Compassionate Life*, Marc Barasch says compassion is the capacity to see *you in me and me in you*.[2] Sin is spiritual blindness – the inability to see you in me, and me in you.

This is what Jesus meant when he said the greatest commandment is to love God and everyone – God in me, God in you, you in me, me in you, God in all of us. Empathy, the seeing you in me and me in you, is the heart of compassion. Because compassion heals separation, compassion lessens everyone's suffering.

Nonetheless, pain in life has a purpose, which is to help us grow. Elisabeth Kübler Ross, who did much work on death and dying, once said, "You will not grow if you sit in a beautiful flower garden, but you will grow if you are sick, if you are in pain, if you experience losses, and if you do not put your head in the sand, but take the pain as a gift to you with a very, very specific purpose."[3]

Julian of Norwich asked God a question. She asked God why, if God was all knowing, God didn't know enough to prevent sin and suffering. God told her that sin is necessary. God also told her not to worry. That over time, everything will work out. The world may appear to be in chaos now, but this disarray is necessary. Everything will work out.

We will not grow unless we break through old patterns, assumptions and blockages. When I face my estrangement and alienation with myself and in my relationships, it's inevitably painful. But when I learn from my experience, I am changed, transformed and enlarged.

Every difficulty we experience is a teaching and reminder that there is only one consolation in life. The purpose of sin is not to create guilt or attract punishment but to remind us of how to live our lives closer to each other and the Holy One, and to teach us how to love.

I live by the mantra, "love is not a feeling, love is not an emotion; it is the awareness that we are all a part of each other, we are always connected."

Love is the awareness that life is perfect unity. Life is harmonious every moment. The puzzle always fits together. It's just that we can't always see it. We are all ignorant – we don't know how to see ourselves as already connected. When we don't have this awareness, we become self-absorbed and separate.

There's a saying that angels can fly because they take themselves lightly. They know how to love and be loved. When we know this, we lighten and open up. When we open up, we become more spacious. There's room in us for others. When we open up we are able to see you in me, me in you. And when we see this we realize that whatever separation we experience with others is created in our own minds.

When I sat down on that plane in Narita airport and realized that I had become the very thing that disgusted me, I smiled. After a while I was even able to laugh at myself. Being able to laugh gave me perspective on myself.

Ogden Nash's poems are nothing if not lighthearted. In poking fun at us, he reminds us not to take ourselves too seriously.

He writes, "The only people who should sin are those who can sin and grin."

Grinning helps us keep perspective even while sinning, I guess.

There is the story of a country pastor who was preaching against the evils of alcohol. As he reached the climax of his sermon, his passion surged. Lost in his own emotion he said, "If I had all the beer in the world, I'd take it and throw it into the river."

Then, with even greater passion, he cried, "If I had all the wine in the world, I'd take it and throw it into the river."

And, finally, he proclaimed, "And if I had all the whiskey in the world, I'd take it and throw it into the river."

Then, trembling, perspiring and spent, he sat down.

In the silence that followed, the song leader smiled timidly and stood up. Then, clearing his throat, he said quietly, "For our closing hymn, let us sing number 365, *Shall We Gather at the River.*"

So when you are experiencing separation, alienation or conflict with another human being – that is to say, when you sin – grin. Don't be so serious. Don't be so self-righteous. Don't take yourself so seriously. Practise laughing at yourself. Laughter will create spaciousness and from that compassion will arise. And with compassion, we can see ourselves in others. You in me, me in you.

That's why I agree with Ogden Nash. When you sin, grin.

[1] Annie Dillard, *Pilgrim at Tinker Creek* (HarperCollins, 1989)
[2] Marc Barasch, *Field Notes on the Compassionate Life* (Rodale Books, 2005)
[3] Sy Safranksky, ed., *Sunbeams, a Book of Quotations* (North Atlantic Books, 1990)

11

The Resurrection of Judas Iscariot

An admirer once approached Mae West and said to her, "I'd give half my life for just one kiss."

Mae West answered, "Then kiss me twice."

Of course it was also Mae West who said, "I generally avoid temptation unless I can't resist it."

Long before there was ever Mae West, there was Judas Iscariot. With one kiss, Judas Iscariot took the life of Jesus. However, Judas kissed Jesus not as an act of love but as an act of betrayal.

The unveiling of the gospel of Judas gave new life to the debate about whether Judas was indeed acting as a betrayer or not. But whatever the motive, the name Judas has become synonymous with betrayer.

Betrayal is an ugly word. But in moments of candour, we have to admit that there have been times when we have betrayed ourselves or others. Perhaps we have kept our mouths shut when we should have spoken. Perhaps we have turned away from those in need when helping out didn't suit us. Betrayal takes many forms.

The lure of 30 pieces of silver comes in a variety of ways. Just think of the powerful calls of money, sex, social approval, or immediate gratification. Refusing to leave our safe cocoon when the needs of the world call us to stretch beyond it is betrayal. And turning away from one's own conscience is a deeper form of personal betrayal.

Sometimes it is only when we are forced to face the consequences that we come to understand the full meaning of the deed. When Judas turned Jesus over to the authorities, the enormity of the deed suddenly hit him. The canonical gospels say that when Judas realized what he had done, he hanged himself.

Everyone I know has met the Judas within in some form. And everyone has had at least one Judas in their life, although most of us have not been betrayed and handed over to the authorities. The betrayals we experience are more mundane and subtle. We think we can count on a friend, but that friend lets us down. We take someone into our confidence and then find our secret is common knowledge. Or we feel that we've been manipulated. It may not happen often, but it happens. Sooner or later a Judas appears in all our lives.

In the lore of the Christian church, Judas becomes a shadow. Following his betrayal of Jesus and suicide, Judas is never mentioned again in the Bible. He is banished from sight and memory. Betrayal belongs in the dark.

It was not only Judas who betrayed Jesus before his crucifixion. These other betrayals were not as dramatic or as severe as that of Judas, but his friends nevertheless turned their backs on him in his hour of need.

In the early morning hours before Jesus was crucified, Simon Peter cowered on a street corner. A woman pointed her finger at him and accused him of being a follower of Jesus. Fearfully, Peter responded, "I don't know what you are talking about. I never saw him before."

Peter is then asked this question on two more occasions, and both times he says he has no idea who Jesus is.

In John's gospel, Jesus appears to the disciples one morning after the Resurrection as they are fishing. Together they clean and cook the fish and eat breakfast. As they finish eating, Jesus turns to Peter and asks, "Do you love me?"

"Yes, you know I do," answers Peter.

Again Jesus puts the question, and again Peter replies, "Yes, of course."

And yet a third time Jesus inquires, "Do you love me?" and for a third time Peter answers, "Lord, you know everything, and you know I love you."[1]

As the resurrected Jesus makes a triple inquiry as to whether Peter loves him, Peter is forced to face his triple denial. Perhaps Peter blushes in embarrassment and shame as his betrayal is brought out into the open.

On the other hand, now that everything is out in the open he is able to breathe a sigh of relief. He knows Jesus has forgiven him.

It is Judas alone who is never given the opportunity to renew, redeem, or restore himself.

The 19th-century British poet Robert Buchanan wrote an epic poem about Judas Iscariot. *The Ballad of Judas Iscariot* tells that after his betrayal of Jesus, Judas sinks into a deep depression and commits suicide. His soul wanders around the universe carrying his body, searching for a place to lay it down.

The soul of Judas carries his body to hell, but hell turns him away. He tries to give the body back to the earth, but the earth refuses. Nowhere in the universe is there a place for the soul of Judas to find relief from carrying around this body of a betrayer.

At last, in a nameless region of darkness, ice, and snow, the soul of Judas sees a lighted hall and the shadows of people moving within. He lays his body in the snow and runs back and forth outside the windows. Judas does not know it, but inside Jesus is sitting at his table with guests.

Buchanan's poem continues:

"Oh, who is that," the Bridegroom said,
"Whose weary feet I hear?"
'Twas one look'd from the lighted hall,
And answered soft and slow,
"It is a wolf runs up and down
With a black track in the snow."

The Bridegroom in his robe of white
Sat at the table-head –
"Oh, who is that who moans without?"
The blessed Bridegroom said.

'Twas one looked from the lighted hall,
And answered fierce and low,

"Tis the soul of Judas Iscariot
Gliding to and fro."

'Twas the soul of Judas Iscariot
Did hush itself and stand,
And saw the Bridegroom at the door
With a light in his hand.

The Bridegroom stood in the open door,
And he was clad in white,
And far within the Lord's Supper
Was spread so broad and bright.

The Bridegroom shaded his eyes and look'd,
And his face was bright to see –
"What dost thou here at the Lord's Supper
With thy body's sins?" said he.

'Twas the soul of Judas Iscariot
Stood black, and sad, and bare –
"I have wandered many nights and days;
There is no light elsewhere."

'Twas the wedding guests cried out within,
And their eyes were fierce and bright –
"Scourge the soul of Judas Iscariot
Away into the night!"

The Bridegroom stood in the open door,
And he waved hands still and slow,

And the third time that he waved his hands
The air was thick with snow.

And of every flake of falling snow,
Before it touched the ground,
There came a dove, and a thousand doves
Made sweet sound.

'Twas the body of Judas Iscariot
Floated away full fleet,
And the wings of the doves that bare it off
Were like its winding-sheet.

'Twas the Bridegroom stood at the open door,
And beckon'd, smiling sweet;
'Twas the soul of Judas Iscariot
Stole in, and fell at his feet.

"The Holy Supper is spread within,
And the many candles shine,
And I have waited long for thee
Before I poured the wine!"

"I have waited long for thee, before I poured the wine." The soul
of Judas finds rest in the tender and forgiving embrace of Jesus.
For Judas, this is heaven.[2]

People often speak about heaven as the place where they
will be reunited with deceased loved ones. Believers in heaven
assume that when they arrive there, they will see the people
they have known and loved on earth.

But the heaven to which Jesus points is a place where we are reunited with strangers and betrayers as well as with loved ones. The heaven to which Jesus points is the space within ourselves that makes room for those who threaten us, for those who are different, for those who have betrayed us. Hell is living with a heart armoured in fierce resistance. Heaven is where the heart is infinitely spacious.

Heaven is where Judas is not only welcomed but fed.

What might Jesus say today about the nature of heaven? Perhaps he would tell us that heaven is not lined with golden streets, but golden Buddhas. Maybe Jesus would tell us that heaven is full of Muslim mosques and Hindu temples, Sikh gudwaras and a magnificent image of the great Goddess giving birth to the universe. Jesus might even point out the atheists' atrium, and laugh at the joke that everyone is there!

We think heaven will be different from earth. But everything Jesus describes as being in heaven is found here on earth. Everything there is here, and everything here is there. In heaven, we learn that everything that is foreign, incomprehensible, and odious, and everything that we try to push away as unacceptable, is eternally within God. Jesus says to Judas, "This is heaven, and you can live in heaven on earth. Heaven is not a place, it's a state of consciousness, it's a way of life."

Here comes Judas, again, and again, and again. He represents everything we seek to turn away from, everything we seek to deny, avoid or defend ourselves against. Judas may have been an historical character or not. It doesn't matter. The real Judas appears within us in many guises. He appears day after day, week after week. In our anxieties, our fears, our inadequacies, our anger, and our jealousy, Judas appears again and again.

In the Buchanan poem, Jesus embraces Judas and says, "I have waited long for thee."

What if there is a Christ in every Judas, a Judas in every Christ? What if there are no such things as outsiders and insiders? What if the spiritual challenge is to allow the Christ within us to embrace the Judas before us?

What if there is no separation?

---

1   John 21
2   Morton Kelsey, *The Other Side of Silence* (Paulist Press, 1995) 347

12

Living beyond Our Belief Systems

··· ❦ ···

In Nigeria in ancient times, there was a God called Edshu.
It is said that this God constructed a big hat. This wonderful
hat was divided right down the middle. The left side was brilliant
blue and the right side was flaming red. As Edshu walked down
the road wearing his hat, those on his right saw the hat as
flaming red, while those on his left saw it as brilliant blue. All
were equally astonished to see God walking down the road.

After Edshu had passed by, everyone converged in the middle
of the road to talk excitedly about seeing God. Some commented
on God's beautiful red hat. Immediately, others argued that the
hat was blue. There was disagreement. Voices got loud and angry
and fist fights began to break out.

While the people were quarrelling, Edshu appeared again, still wearing his hat. This time he stopped and stood in the middle of the road. And when everyone had gathered round, Edshu slowly turned to the left. Then he turned to the right. The two-coloured hat was revealed to all and sundry, and they saw how they had been fooled. They began to laugh at the joke of it. They suddenly "got" the punchline, that there is no belief system large enough to contain the whole truth.[1] Belief systems take us only so far.

We like to think we have life figured out. But life is a trickster god wearing a multicoloured hat. Inevitably something happens to test our beliefs. Someone who sees a different colour of hat than we do shows up. Someone we love very much dies suddenly. We are diagnosed with an aggressive cancer and given two months to live. An earthquake shakes our life apart. A hurricane blows our red hat away.

A number of years ago I sat with a woman named Mary, who was diagnosed with advanced cancer. When she first received the diagnosis, she panicked. Then, as reality set in, she began to utilize every healing resource available. She used Western medicine's latest technologies as well as many different alternative treatments.

Her cancer went into remission.

She said to me, "I believe I have defeated this cancer. I believe that if I do everything in my power to get well, and trust with my whole heart that miracles come from God, I will be cured. I am 100 percent certain I am going to beat this."

Unfortunately, eight months later, she found out that the cancer had metastasized. Prior to this, Mary had held great faith in her ability to overcome the disease. So when she found out that it had come back, she understandably went into a tailspin. She died six months later.

However, during those final six months of life, Mary changed. She gave up on results and on changing the outcome, and put her entire attention on being fully present in the life she had. About a week before she died, she said to me, "It's okay now. I feel I'm being held in the everlasting arms of God. I can feel the embrace. I am not alone and I am not afraid."

Mary's story highlights several different systems of belief.

First, she believed she could not get terminal cancer. She convinced herself of a fantasy. She believed it could not happen to her.

Then, as it became obvious that the diagnosis was fact, Mary was forced to a deeper level. She shifted her attention from believing only in what she wanted (not having cancer) to believing in the reality of the situation. This was a rude awakening. When she got over the shock of it, she came to believe once again that she was in control. She believed she could defeat the cancer. Mary took charge of her life and developed faith in the nostrums of magic bullets and positive thinking.

Later, when the disease came back with a vengeance, she was forced to adapt once more. She could no longer deny the truth of her illness by believing in a cure. With nowhere to turn for another belief system to save her, she went within. Rather than trying to cure her body, she put her attention on healing her life.

By being forced more deeply into her own experience, Mary found something beyond a mere belief system. She opened to her inner heart, her soul.

The self that Mary came to know as she was dying was the self that rests in the Divine. It was her true self. The process of letting go of her fear, her defences, and her shoulds, coulds, and woulds allowed her to open to herself, her friends and her family members. The Holy appeared to her in every person who walked through her door. The fear, anxiety, and desperation were gone.

Mary's body was not cured but her life was healed. This healing came not from what she believed but from what she experienced.

The early 20th-century medical missionary and theologian Albert Schweitzer worked with the poor, the sick, and the dying for many years. He became convinced that what finally restores people to health or restores their lives to wholeness is what he called "the doctor within."

Conventional Christianity says that healing, hope, and wholeness are transmitted externally. Conventional Christians are told to believe in the authorities, such as the Pope, the church, the Bible, the doctrine, and the creeds, rather than in their own experience.

Buddhist writer Sharon Salzberg offers that "...the tendency to equate faith with doctrine, and then argue about terminology and concepts, distracts us from what faith is actually about. In my understanding, whether faith is connected to a deity or not, its essence lies in trusting ourselves to discover the deeper truths upon which we can rely."[2]

Real spiritual strength comes not from any external authority but rather from our own inner authority, the authority of our own experience, the teacher within.

Ram Dass' teacher, Neem Karoli Baba, said that he loved to go to hospitals and graveyards because they always brought out God in people. If you have spent much time with those who are sick or in grief you know what Baba meant. When our defences melt away and there is nothing left to do, and no precious belief to sustain us, we realize that there is nowhere to turn but to the One in whom we live and move and have our being.

It is true that belief systems handed to us by others can be helpful to some degree. William Sloane Coffin once observed that legalistic codes and belief systems are like sticks that support tomatoes as they grow. The sticks have a purpose. They do hold things up. But the sticks are not alive. A tomato grows because of the sun, water, earth and air. The tomato gets its life not from some inanimate object but from the energy of life itself.

It is one thing to say, "I believe in the Ten Commandments – they tell me not to kill anyone so I won't."

And it's another thing to say, "I know killing is the most extreme form of violence there is, and I'll have nothing to do with it. Moreover, I will not knowingly do violence to another living being."

If we say we won't kill because of a rule handed down by someone else, then we are following an external belief system. If we say we will not partake in any form of violence because we know violence is wrong, then what we are saying comes from a deeper place (perhaps from the teacher within?). To live into our own truths is to live beyond the belief systems we've been handed. It is to go beyond the minimum. And we don't have to be on our deathbed to go beyond the minimum.

In our culture, Jesus is often presented as someone who can take us wherever we want to go. There is one proviso, however. We must buy the whole bundle of beliefs that make up the Jesus package. It's all or nothing. If we don't believe in a "virgin birth," then we can't possibly believe that Jesus was the Son of God. If we don't believe that his death on the cross saved believers from their sins, then we must think that Jesus was a mere human being and we just don't get it. If we don't interpret the Bible literally then we don't understand what the Bible is really saying, or accept it as the authoritative Word of God. Unless we swallow the complete Jesus package hook, line and sinker, we are lost.

But what are the "right" things to believe and who has the authority to decide? Who do we trust to decide what or who is on the list? How can one person claim to be any more inspired by the Holy Spirit than another? Who has it figured out enough to insist on being right?

Christ is the Christian word for the divine energy that connects everything. In Buddhism this power is called the *Buddha*. In Judaism some call it the *Shekinah*. In Hinduism it is called the *Atman*, in Sikhism it is known as *Naam*. Every religious and spiritual tradition understands this power in a unique way, and this only magnifies the mystery of it.

Christ power always manifests itself as love, compassion, non-violence, forgiveness, perfect understanding, and peace. And it would transform the world if each one of us would recognize that we all have the same mission in life; that is, to be Christ, or Buddha, or a rose by any other name.

Christ power is divine and holds everything in the universe together. Sometimes known as the cosmic or universal Christ, this Divine energy is what becomes incarnate in physical forms. It was first revealed in a Mediterranean peasant named Jesus but it is not limited to Jesus.

Christ is not a particular identity but a universal power. This power came through but was not limited to Jesus. This Christ power is neither male nor female. It is a compassionate life-giving power that comes through each and every human being. Christ power breaks through whenever we feel closeness, connection, or unity with another living creature. This Christ energy is what gives us the capacity for compassion. Christ is the divine river that flows through us all.

Christ, like love, is a process. To relate to Christ as an external truth is to be ingested and consumed. Relating to Christ as an external truth or redeemer turns Christ into a product. Holding a belief is not the same as living the power of it.

Meister Eckhart spoke of the real way to know Christ when he wrote, "Do you want to know where to find Christ? Your soul is Christ."[3]

Eckhart suggests that the likeness of God is planted within the soul like a seed. It grows in us.

> The seed of God is in us. If the seed had a good, wise and industrious cultivator, it would thrive all the more and grow up to God whose seed it is, and the fruit would be equal to the nature of God. Now the seed of a pear tree grows into a pear tree, a hazel seed into a hazel tree, the seed of God into God.[4]

We are born with Christ in us. Our task, as Eckhart puts it is to be good, wise and industrious farmers of this inner seed. If we are the least bit open, it grows. This Christ power doesn't come to us from outside. It happens through us, arising from within.

This Christ power is an inner whisper. It is the still, small voice that speaks to us in every encounter, every relationship, from every being. It is the teacher and doctor within. It is the power to understand without criticizing, to perceive without passing judgment, to comprehend without analyzing.

Just imagine how Christianity would be different if we lived beyond our belief systems and knew to be Christ rather than a Christian.

[1]   Joseph Campbell, *The Power of Myth* (Anchor Books, 1998) 275
[2]   Sharon Salzberg, *Faith* (Riverhead Books, 2002) xiii
[3]   Matthew Fox, *Breakthrough: Meister Eckhart's Spirituality in New Translation* (Image, 1980)
[4]   Ibid

13

They Won't Arrest You for

Divine Intoxication

··· ❧ ···

I realize that for some, taking Communion is simply a gross idea. On the surface, it can be seen as a sort of a cannibalistic ritual. And even if the words of Jesus are taken symbolically, many people have trouble swallowing the metaphor.

Many scholars question whether the story of the Last Supper is even historical. We don't know if Jesus had a last meal of bread and wine with his disciples. If he did have a meal, it could have been brunch for all we know. This story may simply be a legend that developed decades after the crucifixion. However, the story clearly served the purpose of creating a unifying ritual for the scattered and diverse Christian community of the first century.

Although we do not know what the facts are around the Last Supper, we do know that Jesus ate many meals in public. We know that he would break bread with anyone who wanted to sit down and share a meal.

The gospels say that Jesus ate and drank with lepers, sinners, and prostitutes. These days, two millennia removed from the folkways and mores of first-century Palestine, it is difficult for us to grasp the significance of this. At that time, there was no public act more intimate than to share food with another person. To eat with a leper was to declare one's self a leper. To eat with a prostitute was to prostitute one's self. To eat with the religiously unclean was to become an outcast. So the table fellowship practised by Jesus was truly revolutionary and subversive. And the authorities viewed it as a desecration.

Why did Jesus do it? Why did Jesus behave so offensively to the powers that be? Was he trying to bring them down? Was he, as liberation theologians suggest, taking the side of the poor because God always takes the side of the poor and oppressed? What motivated his behaviour?

According to the gospels, the scuttlebutt among the religious elite was that Jesus was a glutton and drunkard and a sinner himself, not just an associate. But truth be told, it's not unusual for great spiritual teachers to appear a little too happy, giggly or simply "lit up." They are high on Divine intoxication. Other people also seem to "light up" when in their presence. Spiritual bliss is more contagious than laughter.

While serving as the Chair of the Parliament of the World's Religions, I had the pleasure of leading a small delegation of trustees to Dharamsala, India for a meeting with His Holiness, The Dalai Lama. At the end of the two-hour meeting the participants all exchanged gifts. As I walked out of the office, I realized that I was in a completely blissful state of mind. I have also had this experience on several other occasions after having been in the presence of great spiritual teachers. The Dutch Roman Catholic scholar Edward Schillebeeckx wrote that, "being sad in Jesus' presence was an existential impossibility."[1]

We all know there are some people in whose presence we just feel better about ourselves. I'm guessing that Jesus was one of those people, one hundred times over. If he lived in India today, he would be called *sat guru*, *sat* meaning "true" and *guru* meaning "light giver."

To Sufis, the *sat guru* is called a cupbearer. A cupbearer is a spiritual teacher so full of Divine love that when eye contact is made, the other person is immediately filled with Divine love. It is as if Divine love pours from the cupbearer's eyes into the eyes of the other and that person is filled to the brim with the wine of Divine love. The eyes are the window to soul, as they say.

So why *did* Jesus behave so outrageously, eating and drinking with outcasts and spreading love and mercy without qualification? I would say that in the long tradition of great spiritual teachers he was intoxicated, not with the fruit of the vine, but with the nectar of the Spirit. He was *sat guru*, cupbearer, in whose presence one's own cup of life is drained clean and then refilled completely and exclusively with intoxicating Divine love.

Love intoxicates as nothing else can. Intoxication with alcohol or drugs will give us a momentary lift that gradually disintegrates into foggy confusion or sleep. The intoxicating properties of love have the opposite effect. We are awakened. We fall in love and come out of numbness into consciousness.

When we fall in love, we often find ourselves feeling as though we have never been so alive. The intoxication of love puts us in our lives as never before. Falling head over heels in love puts us into an altered state of consciousness. Nothing can bring us down. When something negative happens, the love that fills us keeps us from getting hooked by negative events.

The only thing more intoxicating than the wonder of falling in love with another being is the direct experience of being filled with Divine love. When this happens, we can say with the psalmist, "My cup overflows."

And when the cup of our life is filled with Divine love, all fear disappears. Being filled with perfect love leaves no room for fear.

Julian of Norwich uttered the now famous, "All will be well, all will be well, every manner of thing will be well."[2]

It is intoxicating when we realize in our depths that all will be well, no matter how difficult the moment or how deep our pain. All will be well, no matter what. Everything may fall apart around us, but in our innermost heart, in the soul, we know there is nothing to fear.

And what we all want is nothing to fear.

One of my all-time favourite stories is about Saint Francis of Assisi, to whom the well-known *Prayer of Saint Francis* is attributed.

It is said that when Francis was young man, before his transformation, he would wander the countryside. In those days the disease of leprosy was not uncommon.

Given their grotesque appearance and the odious stench that accompanied their deteriorating skin, lepers were usually banished to the countryside. Their only real source of income came through begging. People would toss something to them from a distance and then run off.

It turns out that young Francis had lepro-phobia. Whenever he saw a leper he would go berserk with fear or anger. He hated the sight and stench of lepers. He couldn't bear the thought of being near a leper, let along actually touching one. Most of all he feared the possibility of contracting leprosy and becoming that which he detested.

One day as Francis was travelling out in the country, a group of lepers appeared. Francis shivered with fear and turned away. But one of the lepers walked toward him, calling out for mercy and compassion. The leper came close enough for Francis to see him. Francis glanced at him fearfully, and was astonished at what he saw. He saw not the face of the leper, but the face of Christ.

Francis was completely filled with love and compassion. He lost it. He couldn't help himself. He rushed to the leper and embraced him, even kissing him on the mouth. In that instant, Francis became intoxicated with Divine love. And once filled with the divine nectar of bliss, there was no one and nothing left to fear.

We all have moments of seeing beyond this veil of tears. We have moments in which everything appears beautiful, elegant, and perfect. We have glimpses of the mystery that supports all of life. All will be well, every manner of thing will be well. Or better yet, everything is already well, if only we have the eyes to see.

Divine intoxication clears things up. Resting in God gives us clarity. It allows us to see life as it really is: whole and holy, a perfect unity. And Jesus is an enduring reminder that Divine love flows from God through us to each other. The Jesus who ate and drank with everyone was really sharing Divine love, not just bread and wine.

I like to think that the bread and cup of Communion remind us to open ourselves to Divine love in everything. Every crumb or drop of love is Holy nutrition. Every drop of love opens us to *real* communion. Real communion is not an outward act but an inner experience. Real communion is Divinely intoxicating. Alighieri Dante wrote:

> The love of God, unutterable and perfect, flows into a soul the way that light rushes into a transparent object. The more love that it finds, the more it gives itself, so that, as we grow clear and open, the more complete the joy of loving is. And the more souls who resonate together, the greater the intensity of their love, for, mirror-like, each soul reflects the other.[3]

As we become intoxicated with the Divine, love overflows from us and spills out everywhere. What the world needs now is Divine intoxication.

[1] Hans Kung and Edward Schillebeeckz, *Consensus in Theology?* (Westminster Press, 1980)
[2] Edmund Colledge, O.S.A. and James Walsh, S. J., *Julian of Norwich Showings* (Paulist Press 1978)
[3] Alighieri Dante, *The Love of God, Unutterable and Perfect*, from *Divina Commedia*, as quoted in *Into the Garden; A Wedding Anthology; Poetry and Prose on Love and Marriage* by Robert Hass and Stephen Mitchell (eds.) (HarperCollins)

PART III

Spiritual Life Is Real Life

... ❧ ...

There is no one here but us chickens.

~ Annie Dillard, *For the Time Being* (Knopf, 1999)

Then it was as if I suddenly saw the secret beauty of their hearts, the depths where neither sin nor desire can reach, the person that each one is in God's eyes. If only they could see themselves as they really are. If only we could see each other that way there would be no reason for war, for hatred, for cruelty...I suppose the big problem would be we would fall down and worship each other.

~ Thomas Merton

14

God and Caesar – Religion and Politics

Some of us believe that God and Caesar, or religion and politics, should remain forever separate.

After all, the doctrine of separation of church and state means just what it says. The law clearly prohibits religious organizations from supporting or opposing a political candidate or political party. Woven into our cultural identity is the separation of God and Caesar, religion and politics, church and state. And this is as it should be.

However, there can be no denying that the success of the civil rights movement was in no small part the result of the commingling of religion with politics. And morality, religion, and politics are back in the news now as we watch the Christian right pursuing its own recipe for success.

Whereas the civil rights movement was all about expanding rights and increasing freedom, the Christian right seeks to limit rights and restrict freedom. Whether it's taking away a woman's right to choose abortion, abolishing the prospect of same-sex marriage, or working to fill the judiciary with socially conservative judges, the Christian right seeks to contract, rather than expand, human rights.

In another time, Martin Luther King stood up to those in power and said, "You haven't gone far enough." Today, leaders of the Christian right say those in power have gone too far and given too much freedom to too many people. These are two very different outcomes from the mixing of religion and politics.

The relationship of religion to politics is inexorable and complicated. Ideally, each could act as a balance and check for the other. And realistically, neither wants its power challenged.

The opponents of Jesus once tried to trick him by questioning him about the relationship between religion and politics.[1] They figured that no matter how Jesus answered the question, he'd end up in hot water. Trying to throw him off guard, one of the officials said to him, "We know that you truly teach the way of God. But we were wondering, is it lawful to pay taxes to Caesar, or not?"

Jesus answered, "Why are you testing me? Bring me a coin, and let me look at it." After looking at the coin, he said, "So whose image and inscription is this?"

"Of course it's Caesar's," the official answered.

"Then render unto Caesar the things that are Caesar's, and to God, the things that are God's."

This was the perfect answer. It got Jesus off the hook for a while longer.

When people ask me if religion and politics should mix, I wish I were as clever and clear as Jesus. I wonder how Jesus would answer that question today, given the plurality of religion and the complexity of politics.

When speaking of politics, most people are referring to partisan politics. A *partisan* is someone who is a firm adherent to a party or cause, particularly if they exhibit blind, unreasoning and prejudiced allegiance. Partisan politics faces off partisans of differing views.

Partisan politics has to do with bolstering the power of a political faction. Partisan politics is about keeping "my guys" in power. It's about getting my candidate elected so that my point of view will be represented. Partisan politics seeks advantage over others. Water down the truth if necessary in order to make it palatable and popular. Partisan politics is a contest and the prize is power. Both sides, all sides, seek to hold the reins of power.

The partisan viewpoint is rarely about the big picture. In partisan politics, politicians may promise change but they are rarely willing to initiate any that will risk their hold on power. This is why the partisan point of view is finally about upholding the status quo.

Jesus did not play the partisan game. Jesus was not interested in maintaining the current state of affairs, because it was obvious that the current state of affairs was inequitable.

Scholar John Dominic Crossan argues that Jesus' healing miracles were, like his table fellowship with sinners, subversive acts that challenged the religious and political partisans.

Crossan contends that the intention of Jesus' healing miracles was not personal but social. His healing was not simply the cure of personal, biological conditions. True enough, a person with leprosy was cured of the leprosy, but such people were also deemed unclean in the eyes of society. What Jesus did was not only to cure the disease but also to heal the person from the social isolation created by their disease.

"This is the central problem of what Jesus was doing in his healing miracles. Was he curing the disease through an intervention in the physical world, or was he healing the illness through an intervention in the social world? Jesus thereby forced others either to reject him from their community or to accept the leper within it as well."[2]

Crossan argues that by restoring the unclean ill to their families and communities and thus defying religious purity laws and social constraints, Jesus rejected the status quo of his day. Jesus refused to be co-opted by the lure and power of partisan politics. Intoxicated with Divine love, Jesus lived out a *politics of conscience* that transcended partisanship. He took the larger view of politics, that is, the total complex of relationship of people living in society. And he brought conscience to inform it.

Conscience is difficult to define, but we know it when we see it. And most of us know what it feels like to be pulled by the inward tug to be true not only to ourselves but to truth as we know it.

Throughout history, many have lived out a politics of conscience. When Martin Luther King spoke out for freedom, led the poor people's march on Washington, and addressed the inhumanity of the Vietnam War he was acting out of conscience. He also riled the partisans.

Five days before he was assassinated, Martin Luther King Jr. preached at the Washington National Cathedral. He said, "I believe today there is a need for all people of good will to come to a massive act of conscience and say in the words of the old Negro spiritual, 'We ain't going to study war no more.' This is the challenge facing modern men and women."[3]

It was a massive act of conscience that ended British colonial rule in India in the late 1940s. It as a massive act of conscience that ushered in the Civil Rights Act and brought legalized segregation to an end in the 1960s. It was a massive act of conscience that brought down the Berlin Wall. It will take a massive act of conscience to bring peace to the Middle East, and to bring an end to injustice and the horrific suffering in Africa. It will take a massive act of conscience in today's world to overcome the rampant violence that threatens to destroy us. Current partisan politics are too petty and invested in self-interest to allow an adequate response to the needs of today's world.

A politics of conscience seeks truth, not power. It seeks the wealth of compassion, not the love of wealth. The only demand it makes is that every living being be treated as holy. It requires humility, openness, and a willingness to admit that we may be wrong. A politics of conscience is the politics of the heart.

The Sikh religion maintains that if you can't see God in all, then you can't see God at all.[4] And Czech playwright, poet, and politician Vaclav Havel puts it like this: "Nothing has convinced me that doing what our hearts tell us to do is not the best politics of all."[5]

Christians in Western culture, whether from the Christian right of Pat Robertson or the Christian left of Jim Wallis, often justify their political positions based on what the Bible says. Now, the Bible can act a guide for the conscience. But to elevate it to the status of external final authority is to rob us of our initiative and ability to act creatively and in concert with Divine will. The Bible does have a role to play as we search our consciences but really, when it comes to matters of conscience, the heart is the queen. The Holy One speaks through our heart and our conscience listens and answers.

Living out a politics of conscience requires us to wrestle with ourselves. It's not about saying we know what's right and wrong and then forcing others to comply with our ideals. It's not about looking for the definitive answer in a book or from a leader who will absolve us of personal responsibility. It's about the struggle to seek within ourselves that place of deep connection to all life. It's about recognizing the connection to all of life and opening up in compassion to all beings, especially our enemies.

A politics of conscience is not a program or an ideology. It is a process. It is having the courage to seek the way of the innermost heart and then live with uncertainty and ambiguity. I call it God, but whatever you call it, something opens us to the innermost heart. And if we are open to our innermost heart, there comes an impulse that forces us to struggle with ourselves. The politics of conscience calls us to struggle with our inability to see ourselves as connected to all of life. The politics of conscience does not blame others.

To do the will of God is to bear witness to the truth. As Bill Coffin put it, "...we are all God's children, Christ died to keep us that way. Our sin is putting asunder what God has already joined together."

I believe this is what Martin Luther King meant when he said, "I just want to do God's will."[6] I just want to get out of the way so that God can act.

Here is the true meaning of the politics of conscience. And no one has stated it more clearly than Dag Hammarskjöld. "The more faithfully you listen to the voice within you, the better you will hear what is sounding outside. Only he who listens can speak."[7]

Open to the action of the heart, the politics of conscience is rooted in the unquenchable desire to do God's will. There is a

Divine inner voice that speaks to us, whispering, "Who do you think you are, and what are you doing?" The conscience is always speaking but often we turn a deaf ear.

I reckon that on some days we do God's will and on other days we don't. Beware of those who tell us they are doing God's will so theirs are the standards we should conform to. Beware of those who say they know God's will and so they have the answers.

In my experience, God appears more often than not as a question. The questions come out as, "Who do you think you are, Bob? Who are these others you work with and meet on the street? Who are these who deliver your mail, who beg, or are homeless. Who are you? Who are they?" God appears in disguise in every being and asks us to look at how we are living from our hearts.

The politics of conscience requires the willingness and ability to wrestle with ourselves and God. It's not about thinking we know what's right or wrong and jamming those conclusions down someone's throat. It is the struggle to seek within ourselves that place of deep connection to all of life.

On fairly regular basis someone will approach me and say that Lake Street Church should take a stand on this or that issue. And sometimes it is important for a church or a spiritual community to take a stand on some issue. And sometimes individuals have to work it out for themselves.

In the 1930s as Hitler was consolidating his power in Germany, most Christian churches remained silent out of fear or apathy. Only a handful of churches, known as the confessing churches, stood up in defiance of Hitler. And many in the confessing church paid a dear price for standing up. But Christians remained mostly silent.

Sometimes silence represents a betrayal of the innermost heart. At other times, silence is its requirement. Those in the confessing church believed that silence in the face of Nazism was a betrayal of conscience. Their collective conscience insisted they speak out.

The politics of conscience is not a program or ideology. To seek the way of the heart requires the courage to live with uncertainty and ambiguity.

The night before he was assassinated, Martin Luther King said: "It's nice to live a long life, longevity has its place. But I'm not concerned about that now. I just want to do God's will."[8] Open to the action of the innermost heart, the politics of conscience is rooted in the unquenchable desire to do God's will.

We may say we are certain that we are doing God's will, but really, who knows the mind of God? No one can ever be 100 percent certain of doing God's will. But if we open to the innermost heart, our conscience, we can draw two conclusions. First, deep within each and every one of us, there is an immense longing to feel whole, complete, at one with ourselves and others. Martin Luther King's deep desire to do God's will arose out of this primal human need. If we accept this as true then we understand that God's will is for us to live in peace. And peace requires nonviolence.

Second, when it comes to human beings living human lives, discerning God's will is not one-stop shopping. Discerning Divine will is more like launching on a pilgrimage rather than receiving one simple answer. As we wrestle with our own conscience, platitudes pale.

Regularly, people stop by the church office asking for help. I have the means to help, but a handout is usually not a hand up. And even though I have the means, my resources are limited. Sometimes I look at the petitioner and I know I am being conned. Other times it's not so clear. I want to do God's will, but the problem is that I often think I don't know what God's will is. In the complexities of everyday life the certainty of Divine will often eludes me. In my experience, God's will is not a once and for all answer but an ongoing question. In my innermost heart I know that God wills unity and wholeness. Finding the way is the challenge.

What is true for individuals is true for society as a whole. Life is full of complexity and ambiguity. To do God's will means struggling with ourselves and wrestling with God. I am convinced that people mostly use the scriptures not to know God but defend against God. It's easier to deal with God in our heads, in a book, in a church doctrine than it is to wrestle with the God in our hearts. Maybe to do the will of God is not about being certain we know the one right thing. Perhaps it is simply God's will that we struggle with our deepest ourselves.

This means that when it comes to religion, we don't act out of reflexive ideology. It means that when it comes to politics, we don't act out of self-interest. Maybe the only answer to the question of God and Caesar and Religion and Politics is finding the courage to live with the ambiguity that is real life. The ambiguity that means that sometimes we must stand up, and sometimes it's better to sit down and shut up.

How do we know?

Let your conscience be your guide.

1   Mark 12:17
2   John Dominic Crossan, *Jesus: A Revolutionary Biography* (HarperSanFrancisco, 1994)
3   James M. Washington, ed., *The Essential Writings and Speeches of Martin Luther King, Jr,* (HarperCollins, 1986)
4   This was the motto of Harhajan Singh Kalsa Yogiji, known as Yogi Bhajan. It expresses the Sikh belief that *Naam*, the Word of God, lives in all.
5   Vaclav Havel, *The Art of the Impossible* (Fromm International, New York, 1998)
6   James M. Washington, ed., *The Essential Writings and Speeches of Martin Luthor King, Jr.* (HarperCollins, 1986)
7   Dag Hammarskjöld, *Markings* (Knopf, 1966)
8   James M. Washington, ed., *The Essential Writings and Speeches of Martin Luthor King, Jr.* (HarperCollins, 1986)

15

A Greater Patriotism

··· ❧ ···

Andrew Bacevich is a Vietnam veteran and the author of *The New American Militarism*. His view is that when push comes to shove, the United States relies on military solutions to solve its international problems. The U.S. is trigger happy. Its unprecedented military power is easily accessed and utilized. It is a militaristic nation and it sees force as the most effective means to achieving its goal of making the rest of the world look and act as it thinks it should.

Bacevich points out that in the 14 years between the invasion of Panama in 1989 to the invasion of Iraq in 2003, the United States conducted nine major military actions. When we consider that the U.S. also has 700 military bases around the world, we might agree with Bacevich's term, "the new American militarism."

The U.S. has come to rely on the military not simply for defence but as a means of solving all of its problems. The military has become a proactive means to any end. And although George W. Bush is an excellent mouthpiece for militarism, both major American political parties glorify the military solution. When John Kerry ran for president, he didn't say that the Iraq war was wrong or immoral; he said the war had been mismanaged and ineptly prosecuted.[1]

American militarism is an incarnation of what Walter Wink calls the myth of redemptive violence. "In short, the myth of redemptive violence is the story of the victory of order over chaos by means of violence. It is the ideology of conquest, the original religion of the status quo. The gods favor those who conquer...Religion exists to legitimate power and privilege. Life is combat...ours is neither a perfect or perfectible world; it is the theatre of perpetual conflict in which the prize goes to the strong. Peace through war; security through strength: these are the core convictions that arise from this ancient historical religion, and they form the solid bedrock on which the Domination System is founded in every society."[2]

"The myth of redemptive violence does not listen to God but speaks for God. It misappropriates the language, symbols, and scriptures of Christianity and uses them as a means to dominate. Its God is not the one ruler of all nations but rather a tribal god worshipped as an idol.

Its metaphor is not the journey but the fortress. Its symbol is not the cross but the crosshairs of a gun. Its offer is not forgiveness but victory. Its good news is not unconditional love for the enemy but their final elimination. Its salvation is not a new heart but a foreign policy that serves its own purposes. It is blasphemous. It is idolatrous. And it is immensely popular."[3]

The myth of redemptive violence wears the face of fear and arrogance. Nationalism linked with redemptive violence gave us a "pre-emptive" war in Iraq after 9/11. The myth of redemptive violence allows us to think that when "they" initiate the violence, it's unjustified or an act of terror (or both) and when "we" initiate it, the violence is necessary (albeit regrettable).

The myth of redemptive violence believes that violence is not only fitting (the other side deserves it) but right (God is on our side). Certain forms of violence, such as war, covert assassinations, torture of suspected terrorists, and capital punishment, are accepted as culturally appropriate.

Violence is always the violation of the identity and integrity of another living being, although it takes many forms. The myth of redemptive violence allows us to rationalize some forms of violence while condemning others. We seem to be able to stomach the violence as long as it is not affecting us personally.

My wife, Judy, and I usually travel to her ancestral home in Georgia for Thanksgiving. The cozy one-bedroom cabin in the woods, with views over the foothills of the Blue Ridge Mountains, is the perfect place to spend the holiday.

One year, I stepped out of the cabin at twilight when the dimly lit sky was aglow. A resplendent full moon rose above the foothills. It looked like a luminous crystal ball. As I stood there, from a distance came the sound of honking. The moon became the backdrop for a flock of geese flying in V-formation. The music of their calling and the soft hiss of the air flowing over their wing feathers faded to silence as they turned and vanished from sight.

Then the silence was interrupted by the sounds of shotgun fire. I imagined lifeless geese tumbling from the sky, their voices stilled. During the silence following the gunshots, I felt a little nauseous, and very sad. I reflected on how our world is beautiful and tranquil one moment, and ugly and violent the next.

As I walked back into the cabin, it came to me that people who shoot animals for sport don't usually make a sport of shooting their own pets. I wondered at the difference between shooting a wild and free goose in the sky and a running, barking dog in a field? After all, aren't they all just animals?

Hunters don't usually go home and shoot Fido because Fido is a familiar and beloved member of the family. It is far easier to do violence to a living being if that being is seen as alien, unfamiliar, and separate.

Surrounded by violence in our culture as we are, we have become numb to it. Marshall McLuhan once pointed out that if you could ask a fish what was the most obvious feature of its environment, probably the last thing it would say would be "water." When we swim in it all the time, we just don't notice it. We are so saturated in violence that we as a people have lost our moral compass. If it weren't so tragic it might be funny.

Several years ago a picture of a soldier smoking a cigarette appeared in newspapers across the United States. The soldier instantly became an icon. He became the epitome of "cool." The photo upset a lot of people. And what upset them was that the photograph made smoking look attractive and glamorous.

Naomi Klein commented in an article in *The Guardian*, "That's right: letter writers from across the nation are united in their outrage – not that the steely-eyed, smoking soldier makes mass killing look cool, but that the photograph makes smoking look cool. Better to protect impressionable youngsters by showing soldiers taking a break from deadly combat by drinking water or, perhaps, since there is a severe potable water shortage in Iraq, Coke."[4]

Parenthetically, Klein adds the smoking soldier controversy reminded her of a joke about the Hasidic rabbi who said that all sexual positions are acceptable except for one: standing up, "because that could lead to dancing."

Barbara Fields told me that while she was involved in the planning phase for the Season of Non-violence annual Gandhi/King commemoration, she sought advice from Thomas Keating. She travelled to visit the Christian contemplative in his monastery in Snowmass, Colorado, and asked him if the effort should be called "the season for peace" or "the season for non-violence." She wondered if peace was a more positive and universal word than non-violence.

Thomas Keating sat back saying nothing for quite a while. Finally he said, "Well, everyone's in favor of peace, but not everyone is in favor of non-violence. Isn't that interesting?"

In Luke's gospel, Jesus sees the destruction of Jerusalem as being just around the corner. He draws near the city and weeps. "If only you knew the things that make for peace. But now they are hid from your eyes..."[5]

We can only create the conditions that make peace possible.

If only we knew the things that make for peace.

Bill Ury, author of *The Third Side*, has extensive experience in creative non-violent conflict resolution. Ury says that all forms of violence are comparable to a virus. He likens terrorism to a manifestation of violence that lies sleeping, then wakens and spreads throughout the body and attacks, as if out of nowhere. Terrorism flourishes when the world's immune system is weak. When everyone is paying attention and working together to prevent violence, the social immune system is strong.

Violence prevention requires creatively addressing conflicts in their earliest stages. The way to transform a culture of violence is to alter the climate that allows violence to take root in the first place.

Every person has a role to play in strengthening the social immune system. Every human being can become a peacekeeper, healer, mediator and teacher of non-violent conflict resolution. We can do this in our homes, schools, neighbourhoods, religious communities, and nations. This is an infinitely greater challenge than flying a flag or singing the national anthem on key.

We are now, one and all, being called to a greater patriotism. A greater patriotism transcends the boundaries of a country and its authorities. It's not my family versus your family, my country against your country, or good people against evil people. A greater patriotism understands the Buddhist teaching of dependent origination.

Dependent origination teaches that everything that exists is dependent on something else. Every part of life is dependent upon other parts of life. The universe is a living organism in which each cell works in balance and cooperation with every other cell in order to sustain the whole.

Our individual well-being is dependent on the well-being of others. My interests and your interests are intimately connected. Every action, word, and thought, no matter how slight or inconsequential, has an implication not only for us but also for all others.

From a spiritual perspective, our true country is not the nation we live in; it is the country of the human heart. As Martin Luther King Jr. put it, "We share this garment of mutuality. What affects one of us directly affects all of us indirectly."

Nothing exists in itself, of itself, by itself, or for itself. Healthy self-interest always takes into account the interests of others. A greater patriotism rises above the parochial boundaries of ethnicity, culture, religion, politics and nationalism. Rooted in spiritual truth, a greater patriotism knows there is no such thing as "us" and "them."

Stop killing. Practice non-violence. Take responsibility for the peaceful resolution of conflict.

If only we knew the things that make for peace.

1   Bacevich, Andrew J., *The New American Militarism* (Oxford University Press, 2005) 15
2   Walter Wink, *The Powers That Be* (Galilee, 1998) 48
3   Ibid, 61–62
4   Naomi Klein. *The Guardian*, November 26, 2004
5   Luke 19:42

16

The Hospitality of Heaven Is

a Queer Thing

··· ୨ୡୡୡ ···

My favourite story from the Taoist tradition is that of a Tao master who was sitting naked in his mountain cabin, meditating. A group of Confucians hiked up the mountain to see him with the intention of delivering a lecture on the rules of proper conduct. When they saw the sage sitting naked before them, they were shocked. "What are you doing, sitting in your hut without any pants on?" they asked.

The sage replied, "This entire universe is my hut. And this little hut is my pants. What are you fellows doing inside my pants?"

It strikes me that the controversy over legalizing same sex relationships is akin to the behaviour of the Confucians in this story. Feeling threatened by the reality of gay sexual relationships, many conservative heterosexuals seek to intervene "inside the pants" of gay and lesbian people. This moral rectitude asserts itself when it comes to the legal recognition of gay marriage.

Several years ago, San Francisco Mayor Gavin Newsom announced that same sex marriages were legal in San Francisco. Thousands of same sex couples took the opportunity to have their "forbidden" relationships pronounced whole and holy. It seemed to them that wanting to be married was a natural thing.

Our personal friends Bill and Scott were among the three thousand that were married. Bill writes of the event in an e-mail to family and friends:

> We did what strikes me now, several days later, as if this were the most natural thing to be doing in all the world on this particular Thursday afternoon. Which of course it was. We were pledging vows in a privately public ceremony... I am still brightened by their simplicity, their utter plainness: I do. I do. I will. I will. Yes. Forever. Until death parts us. We kissed each other, hugged a few of our friends and family, took some pictures, and left City Hall as perhaps hundreds of thousands of other couples have done in the past century: married. For our wedding lunch, Scott and I went directly to In-N-Out Burgers, and had double cheeseburgers, shared a basket of fries, and I had a forbidden chocolate shake. The whole blessed day was both graced and utterly unremarkable.

The Christian Right immediately denounced the event as profane. President Bush stated his adamant opposition to gay marriage and pledged support of a constitutional amendment on marriage. Later, a court ruling nullified all of the marriages that took place in San Francisco.

But one court action cannot stem the growing tide of a human rights movement once the genie is out of the bottle. Throughout history we have watched the circle of human dignity and human rights grow larger. People change. Hearts open. Outsiders gradually become insiders as the marginalized are ushered to the centre of the circle of respect. We are beginning to see this happen in the gay and lesbian liberation movement.

The road to true human community is a long and arduous one.

Whenever human beings have been oppressed by the dominant culture, they protect themselves by living a divided life. When they open the closet door and begin to be accepted into the mainstream, they begin to breathe fresh air and come alive. No longer forced to swallow their dignity, they speak with pride about who they are.

Taking pride in one's self is the beginning of healing. Healing begins when we are able to say, "I am somebody" when we have been told that we are nobody, or at least nobody good. Healthy pride begins with self-respect. Healthy self-respect allows doing unto others as we would have them to do us. Healthy self-respect takes pride in the "we" of our shared humanity rather than the "me" of the victimized self. Healthy self-respect allows us to reach beyond ourselves and our own needs and participate in a larger world.

However, healing is not only about "me" and "my" pain. Healing is related to how my community responds to "my" pain. Healing remains incomplete if it stops with the individual. In Chapter 14, I made reference to the healing miracles of Jesus really being an act of healing back into the community from which the diseased person was alienated and not merely a curing of disease. Lesbian, gay, bi-sexual and transgendered (LBGT) people don't need to be cured of their sexual orientation; they need to be healed back into the larger community.

When healing is an act of community, "my" pain and suffering becomes "the" pain and suffering. It becomes distributed so that I don't have to bear it alone. When our experience of pain is purely personal we reduce it to a privatized experience. We think we are in it alone. We believe that no one understands what we're going through. But in openly sharing "my" pain with a loving community, we discover that pain by its very nature is never private. Pain is a human experience and nothing in human experience is foreign to human beings. There is no such thing as "my" pain or "your" pain. There is only *the* pain, and the more we relate to private and personal pain as an expression of *the* pain, the less power pain has over us. Sharing our pain and suffering with other human beings lightens our load. When we share it with others we release it and stop carrying it around.

Healing spreads as the straight community becomes increasingly empathic to the experience of the LGBT community. The group called Parents Families and Friends of Lesbians and Gays (PFLAG) offers forums and open conversations in churches in order to provide education and advocacy for LGBT people. Providing education and advocacy is to reach out in healing to a subculture that has been quietly victimized by the powers that be.

It's the larger community that applies the true balm of healing. Left to ourselves, we can only continue to lick our wounds. Healing into community mirrors the journey from the crucifixion of hellish separation to the joy of resurrection and reconnection. And resurrection and reconnection are made possible only by love.

In biblical Greek, this expression of all-encompassing love is called *agape*.

As Martin Luther King Jr. explained, "*Agape* is an understanding, redemptive, creative good-will toward all (human beings). *Agape* is an overflowing love which seeks nothing in return. Theologians would say it is the love of God operating in the human heart...this is what Jesus meant when he said, 'Love your enemies.' And I'm happy he didn't say *like* your enemies because there are some people I find pretty difficult to like."[1]

The road to human community is arduous.

In the late 1990s, 21-year-old university student Matthew Shepherd was violently killed in an anti-gay hate crime. The story became national news. During the funeral, fundamentalist Baptist preacher Fred Phelps stood outside the church with some members of his congregation yelling abuse and holding up extremely hateful signs. More recently, Phelps and his hostile band of tormenters have shown up to picket funerals of Iraqi war veterans, proclaiming their deaths as a punishment from God because America harbours homosexuals.

I too am happy that Jesus didn't say you had to like your enemies, because I admit that my immediate reaction to Fred Phelps is to tell him to go to hell.

And it interests me that I make the same pronouncement toward him that he makes toward gays and lesbians. Muslim and Christian fundamentalists wish liberal religionists and secularists the same. Everyone is eager to send their polar opposite to hell. Fred Phelps sends me to hell. I send him to hell. How long can this go on?

Why not try something different?

One way to change an outcome is to change the premise. So, Fred Phelps sends me to hell and I send him to heaven. I send him to heaven because I choose to end the cycle of suffering and violence. I send him to heaven because there he will suffer less and perhaps learn that in refusing to cause suffering for others, he will suffer less himself.

When I see heaven through the eyes of Jesus, I see the faces of those who are strange to me. I see those who cause me to recoil in fear, disgust or horror. Jesus showed us a heaven where strangers break bread with strangers.

Jesus welcomed those the world had pushed away. He revered those who were reviled. He cavorted with hookers. He let the crooks and the poorest of the poor into his life. He might well have said, "Look at these strangers. You may think they are strange. But no one is a stranger to God. You are a part of God, and they are a part of God. Heaven is unity. It is separation that is hell."

Jesus shows us how to go to heaven. He shows us that we get there by living as he lived; welcoming the stranger, refusing to accept alienation and living beyond our self-created categories of separation.

Many years ago the Lake Street Church of Evanston opened the one and only homeless shelter for adults on Chicago's north shore. At first we were stretched thin for volunteers. I kept vigil for many nights and came to know many of the homeless people quite well. Day after day I left my comfortable home to go to the stark and somewhat depressing church basement that was the only home those 20 people knew.

Late one night I sat with one of the guests in the shelter, someone I had known for a while, talking into the wee hours of the morning. We were having our usual conversation about life in general and life on the streets, and musing about people doing bad and good things to each other. I felt pity for this man and his situation. My heart went out to him. But truth be told, when I looked at him in his sorry, homeless condition, I felt a little superior. Sitting across from him I was reminded that we lived in different worlds and I knew the world I lived in was better.

But as we went on talking, something strange happened. Suddenly, I looked into his eyes and there was no distance between us. Suddenly, it was as if the two of us were really one person. My ego had been telling me we were separate. Suddenly, I realized we weren't.

And what amazed me most was that, on looking deeply into his eyes, I saw not only him but myself. I saw myself as never before. I understood my own subtle arrogance, the kind of arrogance that hangs in the back of your mind quietly whispering, "I'm better than you. I have the truth and you don't. Thank God I am not like you. Thank God I don't have your karma."

In the flash of that moment, my eye of understanding opened, and I saw my own egotism in its grotesque dimensions. Recognizing this truth in myself, the walls came down. My heart opened, and for a few moments the distance between us completely vanished. In that instant, I knew him as well as I knew myself.

As my heart opened to him I realized that in spite of everything that separated us, we were not strangers but long lost friends. It was heaven on earth.

That's when I realized that true hospitality looks at the stranger and sees nothing strange. It's still easier for me to welcome a homeless person as a friend than it is to welcome Fred

Phelps. But at a fundamental level, they are both strangers and strange. And they are me.

If I look deeply enough it's possible for me to see you in me and me in you. And herein lies the key to the hospitality of heaven. When we are open to another and look deeply, no matter who that "other" might be, we are able to see that the presumed stranger is really no stranger at all. It is in this way that the hospitality of heaven to which Jesus points is so utterly amazing. The hospitality of heaven assumes no strangers.

And the most amazing thing is that in directing us to the hospitality of heaven, Jesus points us not to heaven in the sky but to heaven on earth.

While visiting Japan, my wife Judy and I stayed in a large hotel in downtown Yokohama. As we checked into the hotel it was clear that we were strangers. We could understand about two words in Japanese and I was afraid to speak one of them, fearing that in mispronouncing it I would say something obscene. I felt a little like a bull in a china closet. Fortunately, the concierge and other staff of the hotel extended great hospitality to us strangers.

The French word *concierge* originally meant "the keeper of the candles." In medieval times, the concierge was a person employed by the wealthy owners of large castles. Whenever an event would take place in one of the castles, it was the responsibility of a concierge to light candles and keep them burning. As people moved from room to room, the concierge went before them, welcoming people and bringing the light.

To be a bearer of the hospitality candle is to create an ever expanding circle of welcome that embraces all strangers and shuts no one out in the dark. There's a place for Fred Phelps, for the homeless, for rich and poor and elderly people. Your worst enemy is there. The most disgusting person you can think of is going to heaven. It's an odd thing, but we are all there, especially in our raunchy imperfection. Heaven is in us, and we are in heaven. It's just a matter of waking up.

We are all part of God. We are all part of heaven on earth. And as we become a concierge for the strangers among us, they become a keeper of the welcome light for us.

This is the hospitality of heaven. And it's a queer thing.

---

[1] James Washington, ed., *Martin Luther King, Testament of Hope* (HarperCollins, 1986)

17

Surrender Your Life to Something Greater

There's nothing like a little recognition to make us feel good about ourselves. We have come to think that gaining the recognition of others is the key to living a life of value. Practically every culture worships celebrity. We think that being famous is the epitome of achievement. We all want our 15 minutes (at least) of fame.

Members of Lake Street Church are often greeted at the door with a cheery, "It's nice to see you!" One member, Jim, used to answer, "It's nice to be seen."

This desire to be recognized is innate, which is why our children call out to us, "Hey! Look at me! Watch me!"

Living as we do in a culture of celebrity makes it tempting to believe that having the adulation of others is what makes an important life. It *is* nice to be seen. It feels good to be known. To be seen by others feels like a confirmation of our existence. It's a celebration of the fact that we are alive and that we matter.

Whenever I attend a fundraising event, I marvel at how often people scurry to have their picture taken with the celebrity-in-attendance. We feel important when we are seen and photographed with a celebrity. Subconsciously, we hope that a brush with celebrity will rub off on us and perhaps make us famous. It's easy to confuse a brush with celebrity with a moment of greatness.

That inimitable 14th-century Sufi rascal Nasrudin one day returned to his village after visiting the palace. Everyone gathered around to hear what he had to say about going to see the king.

"I shall be brief," Nasrudin said. "My greatest moment at the royal palace came when the king spoke to me."

The people were overcome with awe and wonder. They whispered to one another, "The king spoke to Nasrudin!"

One by one they walked away, wondering what it would be like to have the king speak personally to them. They felt important talking to Nasrudin because it meant that they were only one degree removed from the king.

One peasant stayed behind after all the others were gone and asked, "Nasrudin, what on earth did His Majesty have to say to you?"

Nasrudin stood up taller. "I was standing outside the palace when the king came out, and he said to me, quite loudly and clearly, 'Get out of my way.'"

Having both the need for self-importance and the need to live a life of greatness can be confusing. The two impulses can feel similar, but they arise from different places.

The need to be important comes from the ego, the separate self. This need to feel important is organic to our humanity. It's universal. I know, because I've seen it in others and I've seen it in myself.

While I was serving as Chair of the Parliament of the World's Religions, I made several trips to India. It was not uncommon to find myself as the featured speaker or a guest of honour at some large gathering. My Indian hosts treated me like a rock star. My presentations were enthusiastically received. Photographers and reporters followed me, peppering me with questions about the inter-religious movement and world peace. My photograph was in the newspaper and I was extensively quoted.

Toward the end of the trip I was beginning to think that perhaps all the attention meant that I really was important. But when my plane landed back in the United States and I walked into the terminal building in Chicago, I was suddenly just another person in a sea of anonymous faces. This was something of a blow to the ego. If it took attention and fame to make me important, I was no longer important.

This is life. We can be important one day, and a mere drop in a very big bucket the next. And when we realize this, we can let go of the need to be important.

We've heard celebrities talk about what it feels like to be in the limelight. They say that at first it feels great. All that personal attention is seductive and intoxicating. Then comes the realization that the moments that feed the ego are hollow and fleeting. The bloated sense of self-importance is just like hot air, quickly gone and just as insubstantial.

True greatness, rather than mere importance, comes from the soul, the source of our connection to others.

This fundamental spiritual truth is one to which Jesus points to in the story of James and John, the sons of Zebedee.[1] James and John go to Jesus and say, "Teacher, we want you to do for us whatever we ask of you."

Jesus answered, "What do you want me to do for you?"

"Grant us to sit one at your right hand and one at your left when you come into your glory," they replied.

Jesus said to them, "You don't know what you're asking. Whoever would be great among you must be your servant."

Arthur Ashe put it another way. He said, "True heroism is remarkably sober, very undramatic. It is not the urge to surpass all others at whatever cost, but the urge to serve others at whatever cost."

It was Mahatma Gandhi who coined the term *satyagraha*, which is a Sanskrit term typically translated to mean "soul force." Rather than submitting to the whims of the current culture and the conditioning of the mind, *satyagraha* means selfless service without any thought of personal gain. A *satyagrahi* is someone who has surrendered to a greater truth than one's own emotions or ambitions.

Dag Hammarskjöld once said, "I don't know Who – or what – put the question, I don't know when it was put. I don't even remember answering. But at some moment I did answer Yes to Someone – or Something – and from that hour I was certain that existence is meaningful and that therefore, my life, in self-surrender, had a goal."[2]

To what exactly was Dag Hammarskjöld surrendering himself? To what did Gandhi, Mother Teresa, and Martin Luther King surrender themselves? At some moment each one answered *yes*. They didn't surrender themselves to being self-important. They didn't even surrender themselves to making a difference in the world. Somehow, at some point, each one surrendered self-will and said *yes*, not to saving the world, but to serving the human race, no matter what.

I often hear people talk about how important it is for them to be true to their feelings. Sometimes I ask, "Which feeling would that be? The feeling now, or the feeling later?"

Spiritual teachers from every tradition tell us that feelings are not the soul's truth. Mostly, feelings are a reaction to the last thing that happened. That said, we must still honour and respect our feelings and the feelings of others. But the surrender to greatness requires us to live out of a deeper place than the feeling of the moment.

Did Martin Luther King go to jail because doing so was what he was felt like at the time? Or did he go out of a deeper conviction? Did Mother Teresa sit through countless cold, dark nights, holding the hands of people who were dying because that's what she *felt* like doing?

Feelings come and go. Tip your hat to your feelings, but take off your coat to living a committed life that is more than a reaction to your feelings. Surrender yourself to something greater, no matter how you feel, and no matter what the outcome.

Victor Frankl was a doctor who was deported to a concentration camp during World War II. He wrote about the many hellish things that happened while he was living in that camp. Reflecting later on the experience, he wrote, "What was really needed was fundamental change in our attitude toward life. We had to learn ourselves, and furthermore, we had to teach those who despaired, that it really did not matter what we expected from life, but rather what life expected from us."[3]

Always, the challenge comes in making the commitment to live in this little moment while giving ourselves over to a greater servanthood.

Let anyone who would be great among you be a servant.

Truth be told, the word servant can be a problem. We are conditioned to thinking of "servant" as synonymous with "slave," but there is a difference. A slave has no option but to follow orders. A servant is always free to say yes or no, free to come and go. A slave is a doormat. A servant is a doorway. The greatness of the servant comes from helping others to discover *their* greatness.

Early on in his life, Gandhi was a leader of the Indian community in South Africa. In the early 20th century he led nonviolent protests against the white supremacist government. He and hundreds of Indians were sent to jail for their resistance.

General Jan Smuts, who was the head of the Transvaal government, really had it in for Gandhi while he was in jail. But Gandhi decided not to become a slave of Jan Smuts. He chose to be a servant. So rather than spending his time in jail fretting and fuming, he spent his time making a pair of sandals for Jan Smuts. When the Mahatma was released from prison, he presented the sandals as a gift to the General, who was deeply touched. The two men became lifelong friends.[4]

There is a greatness that awaits each one of us. No matter whom we are, greatness awaits us. Greatness is a journey of surrender, not a final destination in the limelight.

Say *yes*.

And then, perhaps, ask, "Who is my General Smuts? Who shall I make sandals for?"

---

[1]   Mark 10:38
[2]   Dag Hammarskjöld, *Markings* (Knopf 1964)
[3]   Victor Frankl, *Recollections: An Autobiography* (Perseus Publishing, 2000)
[4]   Ecknath Easwaren, *Gandhi the Man* (Nilgiri Press, 1978)

18

The Devil Is Not What You Think

I sat next to a pleasant and gregarious young woman on the plane coming home from a winter vacation one year. Once airborne, I decided to open my briefcase and review several provocative passages from a book I had been reading.

"What are you reading?" asked my seatmate.

I held up the book, which was *Living with the Devil*.

"Oh," she said, clearing her throat. She then removed her arm from the armrest between us and turned away. That's when it occurred to me that the title of that book might freak out some people. Her reaction was pretty clear, and she didn't look at me or speak to me for the remainder of the flight.

Satan. The devil. Beelzebub. Lucifer. The Ruler of Hell. The very idea of this supreme evildoer is enough to make people turn away in fear. Don't look. Don't think about it.

As Peter says in his Epistle, "Be sober. Be vigilant; because your adversary the devil, as a roaring lion walks about, seeking whom he may devour."[1]

Whether or not you believe in a personification of the devil, this archetype of evil is embedded in the collective subconscious.

I have long believed that the most dangerous of devils is the one who appears as an ally. This version of the devil is the one who appears in the story of Jesus' temptation in the wilderness. In the story, the external wilderness is a mirror of the wilderness within us.

What really happened out there? No one knows, of course. But the story says that after being baptized in the River Jordan by John the Baptizer, Jesus is led by the Spirit into the wilderness. As the memory of this phenomenally blessed experience fades, the arid desert becomes ever more real and present. Ensnared in the solitude, Jesus feels he is going in circles. He asks for answers but gets silence. He asks for a sign but no sign appears. He is alone.

For 40 days and nights, Jesus walks by himself through inner and outer wilderness. Utterly alone, he sits in prayer and meditation hoping for insight, clarity, and an answer. But nothing happens. Shouldn't there at least be a vision after all this time and effort? A burning bush perhaps? A pillar of fire? Where *is* God anyway? What's the point of all this?

Then, voila, Jesus has company. He is no longer alone in the wilderness. Satan has appeared to Jesus, and it is as friend not foe.

In Martin Scorsese's movie *The Last Temptation of Christ*, the devil is portrayed as a cute young girl. This sweet little devil speaks with a beguiling British accent and is so agreeable and disarming that she is difficult to resist. Scorsese's devil is the perfect polar opposite of the old-style male devil with pointy nose and scratchy voice. This charming little Satan appears above reproach. She's an ally. She wants Jesus to realize his goals and she's able to help.

Appealing first of all to Jesus' altruism and compassion, the devil tempts him to turn stones into bread. After all, what better way to proclaim the generosity of God? Feed *way* more than a mere five thousand hungry mouths – feed five million!

Jesus doesn't fall for it.

The cute little devil moves on to Plan B. Now she appeals directly to Jesus' ego. She tells him that God's angels will protect him if he jumps off the cliff. She tells him he is great, he's one of a kind. He and she both know it. The world had a right to know it too.

Again Jesus says no.

At this point the devil goes for broke. She promises Jesus that he can rule the world if he just sticks with her. He'll be installed in the halls of power and he can change the world. He'll be in charge. He'll be the main man. There could be no hunger. There could be no sickness. Jesus can give power to the people. Stick with her and he can accomplish all of his goals right now. No need to wait.

In the 1970s, Flip Wilson had his own television show. Every once in a while he would dress up in drag and say that he was Geraldine. Geraldine was a hilarious character and her trademark was to confess to doing something she shouldn't have done and then blame it on the devil. Geraldine would say, "I couldn't help it. I was powerless. The devil made me do it."

Jesus was no Geraldine. He just said no.

The conventional interpretation of this story of Jesus being tempted in the wilderness is that Jesus was able to resist because he was the unsullied saviour whose purity enabled him to redeem the sins of the world. This conventional interpretation seeks to make the theological point that Jesus was not like every other human being that ever lived. To put a finer point on it, the story says that Jesus was like us in every way except for the most important one – basic human vulnerability. He didn't have an Achilles heel. There was no pulling the wool over his eyes. He was human in every way except that he didn't have any flaws or weaknesses. He was above us.

I have a hard time figuring out what this conventional interpretation has to do with life as I know it and live it. It is hard for me to know what this story actually has to do with me or anyone else for that matter. Saying that the reason Jesus did not yield to temptation was because he was God's son, and thus above being fully human, leaves me a little cold. Am I missing something?

Reading Stephen Batchelor's book opened me to a deeper interpretation of Jesus and the devil. *Living with the Devil* is written by a Buddhist who offers a perspective of the Buddha's struggle with Mara, the Buddhist version of the evil one.

Written 500 years before the stories of Jesus' temptation, the Buddhist story tells how Mara tempts and stretches Buddha in every conceivable way. As in the Jesus story, Buddha is tempted by the seductive idea of being able to save the world. When Buddha resists, Mara harnesses the forces of nature to terrify the Buddha. First there are explosions, then earthquakes, fires, and ferocious storms. Mara was so good with special effects that it seemed to the Buddha as if the world was splitting open. Still the Buddha resists. He continues to remain in a state of equanimity as Mara appears in the form of a giant elephant, a king cobra, and an ox. Mara appears in the natural world in all its glory and horror, says Batchelor. And like Jesus, the Buddha remains unshakeable.

The Jesus and Buddha temptation stories are not exactly the same, yet in both the devil does not try to tempt them toward evil *per se*. The devil, says Batchelor, tempts them to believe that life is a puzzle to be solved. Satan and Mara make the same promise: Do this one thing and everything will be perfect. Here. Believe this, meditate on that and you will find the answer, experience salvation, reach enlightenment. You will get everything you want.

Although written at different times and in different cultures, these narratives point to the same devil. For both the Buddha and Jesus, the devil becomes a projection of the desire to reduce the meaning of life to a formula or fixed remedy in the hope that we will be happy.

This is my personal devil. The devil I know tempts me to believe there is some product I can purchase that will solve my problems. The devil I know tempts me to believe there is one religious belief or spiritual experience I can buy into that will fix me now and forever more. The devil I know seduces me into believing that finding the right answers will finally make me feel all right about myself.

The devil is that which seeks to limit us, confine us, fix our horizons and long for all ambiguity to end. The devil is that part of us that tempts us to believe that there is an explanation for everything if only we knew how to get it. The devil is that part of us that tempts us to jump to conclusions or leap upon answers because conclusions and answers make us feel secure.[2]

I often hear people speak of the spiritual journey as if it were a destination vacation. If we are spiritual enough, we'll get there; we'll arrive and finally get saved or enlightened. We all want certainty. We all want to believe that if we find the right formula, get the right belief, or follow the one true path, everything will turn out exactly as we want it to. The temptation is to believe that it's possible to fix life as we know it, and have it come out our own way. This is the same devil that appeared to Buddha and Jesus.

Hugh Prather wrote, "Jesus' life didn't go well. He didn't reach his earning potential. He didn't have the respect of his colleagues. His friends weren't loyal. His life wasn't long. He didn't meet his soulmate. And he wasn't understood by his mother. Yet I think I deserve all those things because I'm so spiritual."[3]

How different do we imagine life would be if we were perfectly "spiritual"? What is our ideal spiritual destination? What's our real goal? Is it to be free of insecurity, pain and suffering? We all yearn for certainty, safety and consolation. The stories of the Buddha and Jesus remind us we seek these qualities above all others.

Roger Housden tells the story of visiting the maze at Hampton Court, the palace outside London where King Henry VIII spent much of his time. The maze isn't a particularly large one, but it's large enough to get lost in. As Housden walked through it, he was unable to see over the high hedges on either side, and he wandered down clever blind alleys that took him nowhere. After about ten minutes of going in circles, Housden acknowledged that the maze was more complicated than he had anticipated.

He relates, " I came to a standstill somewhere in the middle – at least that's where I thought I was – and realized the aim I had come in with, which was to talk through and out, had evaporated. In its place was simply the sensation of myself going nowhere…and I understood in that moment the deeper purpose of mazes. The true purpose of a maze, it dawned on me – is to a-maze us. It even gave us the word 'amazing'."[4]

Life is amazing and astonishing. The devil in us tempts us to say it's not. We get so distracted by our own agendas that we miss the mystery, the amazement, of life itself. We are so preoccupied with getting life to go our way, or with finding the certainty, that we forget to be amazed with the moment we are in.

Good or bad, painful or joyful, every moment of life is remarkable. Every moment brings astonishment. Every moment is a mystery. The great temptation is to push away the moment we're in and thus deny the amazement, the astonishment and mystery of life.

Yield not to the temptation that there is one right answer for the riddle of life. Yield not to the temptation that you need figure it all out.

As Rabbi Abraham Joshua Heschel said, "Just to be is a blessing. Just to be is enough."[5]

And if we must insist upon a definitive answer, let this be it.

---

[1] I Peter 5:8
[2] Stephen Batchelor, *Living with the Devil* (Riverhead Books, 2004)
[3] Hugh Prather, *Spiritual Notes to Myself* (Conari Press, 1998)
[4] Roger Housden, *Seven Sins for a Life Worth Living* (Harmony Books, 2005) 87
[5] Abraham Heschel, *I Asked for Wonder* (Crossroad, 1991)

19

The Things We Carry Around

There is a story about two Buddhist monks who were journeying home. They came to the banks of a fast flowing river, where they met a young woman who was unable to cross the swift current alone. One of the monks picked her up in his arms, carried her across the river, and set her down safely on the other side. Then the monks continued on their journey, walking together in silence.

Time passed, and finally the monk who had not carried the young woman could no longer restrain himself. He reminded his brother that they had taken vows not to touch women because to do so would arouse desires that could interfere with their practice. The monk went on and on about how it was a mistake to break their holy vows.

Finally the other monk stopped walking and turned to his companion. "Brother," he said, "I left that young woman on the bank of the river hours ago. You are the one who is carrying her."

The things we carry around.

Psychiatrist Howard Cutler, who co-authored *The Art of Happiness* with the Dalai Lama, writes of an encounter he had with a well-groomed, well-dressed, middle-aged man. The man came to the office for his first session with the psychiatrist. He sat down and began answering the standard first-interview questions in a soft, controlled voice.

Then, all of a sudden, the man erupted. "My damn wife!" he exclaimed. "Ex-wife now. She was having an affair behind my back! And I did everything for her. That little slut!"

His voice became louder, angrier and more venomous as he recounted grievance after grievance against his ex-wife. Realizing that he was just getting warmed up and could continue in this vein for hours, Howard Cutler redirected him. "Well," he said soothingly, "most people have difficulty adjusting to a recent divorce, and this is certainly something we can address in future sessions. By the way, how long have you two been divorced?"

The man answered, "Seventeen years last May."[1]

The things we carry around.

Why do human beings create suffering for each other? Why do we lack compassion and empathy for each other? What obstructs our spiritual vision? Why can't we see "you in me, me in you"? What blinds us to simple human decency?

It's a universal truth that the one thing we *all* want out of life is to be happy. It's equally true that every human being suffers.

John's gospel relates the story of the woman caught in adultery. Just as we do today, everyone in this story wants to be happy. But nobody is.

As the story opens, the adulterous woman is surrounded by a group of sober-faced, straitlaced and uptight men who want to stone her to death for committing adultery. The story reflects the heavily patriarchal culture of its time. It is only the woman who is "caught." The sexual nature of the sin reinforces the double standard of men who have all the power. A similar punishment does not apply for them.

Jesus intervenes. Looking at the men, whose hearts are blocked by arrogance and self-righteousness, he asks them, "Are you going to kill this woman for her sin? What makes you think you are any better? Who among you is without sin?"

The men are armed and ready to throw their stones. But in a first-century example of a Third Side conflict intervention,[2] Jesus stands between the accusers and the woman. Again he says, "Come on. Who among you has not broken a law, betrayed a relationship or hurt somebody? Who among you has not told a lie to save face or told a half-truth to cover your back. Who among you hasn't had lust in your heart? Who among you is not self-possessed? Who hasn't committed a sin?"

As he speaks, the men back off. One by one, they drop their stones and walk away.

A mental picture of this scene yields images of men with narrow minds and mean spirits. Being the dominating patriarchy, they want to punish the woman for being a woman, as well as for "committing a sin."

But it is also true that those who wanted to stone her were not born with narrow, hateful minds and cold hearts. They were not born into the world with a superiority complex. Their hateful behaviour was learned. All they really wanted was to be happy and they came to learn and believe that by participating in and maintaining the dominant patriarchal culture, they would be happy. *They came to believe that they could only be happy if they stayed in power.*

This poses some fundamental questions.

It is undeniably true that patriarchy as a system of domination had infected the moral discretion of those men. But where does the idea that it's okay for some to dominate others come from?

There is a story about Yogi Berra being driven around in a convertible with the top down. It starts to rain. Forgetting he's in a convertible, Yogi holds out his hands and feels the wet drops. Puzzled, he asks, "Where is this coming from?"

Like Yogi, we sometimes forget that everything comes from some place. The urge to take on patriarchal values is born out of something, and it is my belief that it comes from a closed heart.

When the heart is closed, the mind can convince itself of anything. We can make anything and everything "all right" if our heart can't speak to us or if we don't hear it. When we shut out the loving murmurs of the heart we can find ourselves doing hateful things to other beings, to say nothing of ourselves.

The dominating patriarchy of the gospel existed because hearts were closed and energy could not be drawn from there. Patriarchy is a symptom as well as a cause. Many, if not all, sufferings arise from a closed heart. And our hearts can close for reasons other than the desire to dominate or get our own way.

It may be that we don't feel safe, that we need to protect ourselves. It may be that we are so self-absorbed that we simply can't make room for another in our heart. There are many ways to wall ourselves off from others and we all do it, one way or another. We feel insecure so we become arrogant. We feel fearful so we become defensive. Marching around in our minds is an army of rationalizations that drive others out of the heart.

And we do all these things only because we want to be happy.

This I believe is the deeper spiritual crisis in the story of the woman caught in adultery. Those men believed they would be happier if they dominated the woman. They believed their suffering would cease once the sinner had been killed.

It would seem that the greatest spiritual challenge in everyday life is to get over our narcissism, our self-absorption, our preoccupation with ourselves. This is the very heart of all spiritual practice and it takes a lifetime. And this is what Jesus was saying to that group of men hell-bent on stoning the woman. He was calling them to a larger self, a larger Truth. He was calling them to look beyond themselves to see the bigger picture. He was asking them to see the commonality, rather than the differences.

The work of spiritual practice is to make us larger than ourselves. It is only when we become larger than ourselves that we can become our true self. The paradox is that the true self is selfless.

In Taoism, there is a saying that the ocean is the greatest body of water on the earth because it is the lowest. Lakes, rivers, and streams all drain into the ocean. The ocean has no boundaries, no dikes to keep anything out. The ocean is acceptance. The ocean is where all the waters of the earth meet. The ocean reminds us that the greater our humility, the greater our capacity to receive. To be great in this way is to empty ourselves of all defensiveness, self-possession and the need to be right. To be great like the ocean is to give up our defences and our judgments and not create any dams around our hearts. To be great like the ocean is to welcome everyone into our hearts.

The ways in which we judge and blame ourselves and others end up taking a toll. We reduce our own suffering by letting go of the poison we carry around. We reduce our suffering and that of the world around us by thinking of ourselves as an ocean, with hearts open enough to hold endless quantities of love and compassion. Be the ocean rather than the stream. Be everything, rather than just our own little self.

Sometimes experiences can crack us open and increase our ability to receive.

Following a visit to my mother just before she died, I found myself carrying around nothing but grief. It was clear the end was near. One day, as I was getting on the plane to return to Chicago, the grief, as grief tends to do, softened my heart. I felt strangely vulnerable, as if I had been opened up. I took my seat on the plane. As passengers went past me down the aisle, I looked at each face and saw in each one an indescribable beauty. It's difficult to convey. But I felt a tender connection to each and every one of them. In some odd way I could see the inexplicably precious being in each human form. I cherished these strangers.

The tears of grief that rolled down my cheeks were watering my joy as well as my pain. Tears of grief and joy come from the same deep place. I felt a profound and mysterious connection with these people I did not know and would never see again. More than anything, I was aware of a spaciousness I rarely experience in ordinary life. Alas, it wasn't long before my softened heart began to harden. Yet the memory of that spaciousness lingers.

The great Tibetan Buddhist teacher Chogyam Trungpa Rinpoche once stood before his class and drew a loose V shape in the centre of a large piece of paper. The ends of the V were kind of flopped out. Turning to his students he said, "Tell me what this is a picture of."

There was silence. Then someone suggested it was a bird in flight. One by one the others agreed. Rinpoche smiled and said, "No, this is not a picture of a bird, it's a picture of the sky with a bird flying through it."[3]

We are the sky, we are the ocean. Events fly through us. If we practice letting go of the things we carry around, we open ourselves to the experience of a grand and wondrous mystery. If we can release the things that blind the heart, we may discover that even ordinary moments become moments of spaciousness and wonder.

In his book *Seven Sins for a Life Worth Living*, Roger Housden describes waking up one morning and looking at this wife lying beside him. He writes, "In a fold of cloth, a few inches away, I could make out the flesh of my wife's upper left arm. I could not see where this hint of a human being had come from, nor could I see where it was going. Questions began to drift through the sky of my mind. Who is this person lying beside me? Where did she come from? How did she come to be here? How did I come to be here?"

These are questions that can open us to the spaciousness of life. Apply the questions to here and now, that person we live or work with, the grocery clerk, our neighbours. How did we come to be here in these bodies, in this life?

Housden says, "I realized then that I truly do not know this person at all. I have lived with her for some years now; I have looked often upon her face and felt more than once an upwelling of joy. But she is more a mystery to me than she ever was."[4]

The more spaciousness that is in us, the less we suffer and the less suffering we create for others. The Sufi mystic Rumi put it like this:

Out beyond ideas
of wrongdoing and rightdoing,
there is a field.

I'll meet you there.
When the soul lies down
in that grass,
the world is too full to talk about.

Ideas, language
– even the phrase "each other" –
do not make any sense.[5]

Where did we come from? We all came from the same place, wherever that is.

Where are we going? We are all going to the same place, wherever that is.

And here and now, what does it takes to make the world within and without a better place? Let go of all the things we carry around and become the ocean.

---

[1] HH Dalai Lama, Howard Cutler, *The Art of Happiness* (Riverhead Books, 1998) 149–150

[2] The Third Side comes from William Ury's book of the same name. There are two sides to every conflict, and it takes a third side to resolve it. (www.thirdside.org)

[3] Sharon Salzberg, *Faith: Trusting Your Own Deepest Experience* (Riverhead Books, 2002) 166

[4] Roger Housden, *Seven Sins for a Life Worth Living* (Harmony Books, 2005) 81

[5] Jalal Al-Din Rumi, *The Illuminated Rumi* (Broadway Books, 1997)

PART IV

This Astonishing, Mysterious Moment

... ❦ ...

i thank You God for most this amazing
day:for the leaping greenly spirits of trees
and a blue true dream of sky;and for everything
which is natural which is infinite which is yes

(i who have died am alive again today,
and this is the sun's birthday;this is the birth
day of life and love and wings:and of the gay
great happening illimitably earth)

how should tasting touching hearing seeing
breathing any–lifted from the no
of all nothing–human merely being
doubt unimaginable You?

(now the ears of my ears awake and
now the eyes of my eyes are opened)

~ E. E. CUMMINGS

20

The Spiritual Purpose of Our Relationships

••• ⚜ •••

The story is told of an American tourist who visited an island in the South Pacific. She happened upon a shop owned by people who were indigenous to the island. She found herself admiring the necklace that the shop owner was wearing. She asked him what the necklace was made of. He replied that it was made of alligator teeth.

"Oh, I see," said the woman. "I suppose that alligator teeth have the same value for your people that pearls have for us."

"Not quite," said the shop owner. "Anyone can open an oyster."[1]

Seeking the spiritual purpose of our relationships is more like opening the mouth of the alligator than the shell of an oyster. It is dangerous. It challenges our complacency. But what a prize there is at the end of it.

There is a story about a couple who, on the occasion of their golden wedding anniversary, found themselves having a very busy day. A non-stop procession of family and friends passed through their home to offer their congratulations. Later that evening, after the commotion had died down, the couple sat together silently on their front porch, watching the sunset and basking in the afterglow of the day.

The husband gazed fondly at his wife and said, "Agatha, I'm so proud of you."

Agatha looked at him. "What was that you said? You know I'm hard of hearing. Say it louder."

"Agatha, I said, 'I'm proud of you.'"

"Oh that's all right dear," Agatha replied. "I'm tired of you too."[2]

In every relationship, there are times when we think we hear what is being said but really we are hearing something altogether different. Relationships can be confusing. We say one thing, the other person hears another. We mean one thing but are misunderstood. Relationship is ambiguous.

In the book of Genesis, there is the story of Jacob meeting with his brother Esau, from whom he has been estranged for many years. There is so much bad blood between the brothers that Jacob worries Esau might kill him, or that he might kill Esau.

The night before their encounter, Jacob is all alone in the desert. A stranger suddenly appears and engages Jacob in a wrestling match. Throughout the night they tussle, neither one prevailing. As morning breaks, the struggle ends in a stalemate. Sensing that his wrestling partner had superhuman powers, Jacob asks for a blessing.

Some commentators think that Jacob was wrestling with God, but most say his opponent was an angel. One rabbinical commentary suggests that Jacob was actually wrestling with himself, and it's this interpretation that rings true for me.

When I'm experiencing tension or discomfort in a relationship, I inevitably realize that I am struggling not with the other person but with myself. This becomes abundantly clear if my relational angst happens to keep me awake at night. I toss and turn and the mind jumps from one thought to another. Unable to sleep, I get up and fret about my relational rupture. Who else do we wrestle with in the middle of the night if not ourselves?

Fearing the worst but hoping for the best, Jacob struggled with himself. Jacob had to stare into the mouth of the alligator in order to seek his pearls of wisdom. He had to face his dilemma as it really was.

We want our spirituality to promise *nirvana* in *samsara*, heaven on earth. Conventional Christianity teaches that God is the way *out* of the alligator's mouth. We are taught that God is the answer to our suffering in that God will get us out of whatever unpleasant thing we're in. If God delivers us, it is a sign that God is near and dear. It is a sign that God loves us. Only believe and God will give you your heart's desire. This is the popular gospel. This is mega church theology.

But in my experience, more than I'd like to admit, God's been hard on me. God hasn't spared me from struggle. More often than not, when I'm tied up in knots, God tells me to wrestle with the knots myself. And I don't believe that this means God does not love me or does not think I am worthy of assistance.

What if God is the unbidden Presence in every relationship? What if God is the still small voice that gives us the courage to face the truth and ourselves, and reminds us to see each other with compassionate eyes? What if the Holy One is the inner nudge that urges us to climb above and beyond our self-imposed limitations? And what if the human spirit is elastic and we are created to extend ourselves beyond our comfort zones?

The spiritual or higher purpose of relationships is to challenge us to become great in the way God is great. And God is great in the way of love.

There is an African word, *ubuntu*, which means that a person can only be fully developed through other people. We experience *ubuntu* through being stretched in our relationships. We can't grow if we sit in isolation and seclusion. We experience *ubuntu* and the gift of becoming a person through other people. Whenever we climb above our picky little selves in our relationships and truly hold the other in our hearts, we see that the value of "we" is greater than the value of "me."

To find the spiritual purpose of relationship requires courage. Living authentic relationship requires a willingness to climb on the cross of the moment and acknowledge what is actually being said. Yet we usually hear what we want to hear. We want other people to see the light, as long as it is our light. But in order to truly honour and respect our relationships, we are required to allow our illusions to die.

It is often said that people resist change, but it's truer to say that we resist being changed. The mind is conditioned to protect, defend, and deny. W. H. Auden wrote that, "We would rather be ruined than changed. We would rather die in our dread than climb the cross of the moment and let our illusions die."[3]

In our relationships, the mind is always moving. Like the proverbial monkey jumping around or the dog on a leash yanking us about, the mind is constantly in motion. And it gets in the way. When our mind is leaping about we aren't present in our relationships.

Two Zen monks were having an argument about a flag hanging from a flag pole. One said that the flag was moving. The other insisted that the wind was moving. It just so happened that a great Zen master was walking by and overheard their argument. Stopping in front of the two monks he said, "Not the wind, not the flag; your minds are moving."[4]

Thoughts and feelings come from the mind and the mind is always in motion. When it comes to our relationships, the mind is an exacting accountant. It is always keeping score, adding and subtracting and watching the balance. You give to me, I give to you, but how much, and do I have enough myself? If we come across someone who seems to have nothing to offer us, then the mind tries to convince us there is no reason for a relationship. It doesn't take the value of an alligator tooth necklace into account.

There is a story about a farmer who realized he was becoming too old and too tired to keep working in the fields day in and day out. He knew that his son was very anxious to have the farm as his own, so he decided that he would give the farm to his son before he died.

The next day as they sat together at the breakfast table, the old farmer looked into his son's eyes and said, "I am not going to wait until I die to give you your inheritance. All of this is yours now. I am giving everything to you."

The son was overjoyed to be the new owner of the land. Jumping up from the table, he embraced his father. Then, full of renewed energy, he ran out the door to work his first full day on what was now his farm.

The father, relieved and happy for his son, went out on the porch and sat in the shade as his son worked in the fields. Day after day this scene was repeated. Weeks, then months passed. The father watched his son working so hard and felt very proud of him.

But as the son toiled in the fields, he watched his father sitting on the porch and began to feel resentful. His father just sat there, draining his hard earned money.

Finally, the son's resentment reached the point where he convinced himself that they would both be better off if his father was no longer around. He built a box on wheels, complete with a lockable lid. When it was complete, he rolled the cart over to the porch and asked his father to get in. The old man didn't question him as his son helped him into the box and began to push the cart. He pushed it a very long way, down dusty roads and over fields, until finally he stopped at the edge of a high cliff.

As the son got ready to release the cart over the edge of the cliff, he heard knocking coming from inside the box. He stopped in mid push. He heard his father whisper from inside, "Son, I think I know what you are doing. And I understand. I know I have become a terrible burden. But be sensible. Open the cart and throw me out. Keep the cart. Your children might need it."

Those who cause me the most grief are my greatest teachers, provided I can get over being exasperated and remember to work on myself. A difficult or challenging person is always a great gift from God if we have the eyes to see it. Rather than pushing others over the cliff, we can allow ourselves to be stretched and listen for their wisdom. We can allow ourselves to see ourselves in them, and them in us.

The Rabbi of Berdichev, who was a legendary 19th-century mystic, was called the Master of the Good Eye. He saw only the good, the best, and the holiest qualities in people. [5]

Learning to see with the Good Eye is a challenging spiritual practice, but it works. The miracle is that seeing others as they really are helps us to see ourselves as we really are.

Ubuntu. The spiritual purpose of our relationships is to let others take us where we cannot go by ourselves. By stretching beyond ourselves we return to ourselves.

In this way, seeking the spiritual purpose of our relationships is a little like opening the mouth of an alligator. What a challenge.

But oh, those beautiful teeth.

[1] Anthony De Mello, *The Heart of the Enlightened* (Image Books, 1989)
[2] Ibid
[3] W. H. Auden, *Collected Poems* (Vintage, 1991)
[4] Paul Reps, ed., *Zen Flesh, Zen Bones* (Anchor Books, 1989)
[5] Marc Barasch, *Field Notes on the Compassionate Life* (Rodale Press, 2005)

21

Life Is but a Dream

By my calculation I have preached over 1400 sermons. Having to preach so many sermons to the same audience may well be the cause of a recurring dream that I have.

The dream theme is constant, although the circumstances may change. I am always at home (where I write sermons) when suddenly there is an emergency. Desperately I call out for help. I dial 911 and the operator answers. I open my mouth to ask for help, but I can't speak. I strain to push the words out, but only raspy, squeaky sounds come out. I run to the front door in a panic. People are passing by as I open my mouth to scream for help, but no matter how hard I try, no sound comes out.

Then I wake up sweating and feeling anxious.

I only have this dream when I am struggling to write a sermon. When I can't find the right words, or when I'm not sure what it is I want to say, I dream that I can't speak. I open my mouth but words don't come out. I strain to speak, but I am voiceless. I think, oh no, what if this is it? What if I have finally run out of words? What if I have nothing to say?

One day it occurred to me that the scenario played itself out whether I was awake or asleep. When I am struggling to write a sermon, I can't find my voice. No matter how much I try to express myself, the words won't come, either in my dream or at my desk in the morning.

So what is the difference between not finding my voice in a dream and not finding it when I'm awake? Is it a dream only while I am sleeping? Am I having a dream when I'm awake? Am I awake in my dream?

Many of us have had the experience of awaking from a vivid dream or nightmare and being certain that what we dreamed really happened. Then, as we awaken more, we realize we were only dreaming. It didn't really happen. Or did it?

We can have the reverse experience too; dreamlike moments even though we are awake. One day, while holding my grandson Kai on my lap, I had a waking dream. As if it were yesterday, I remembered sitting on my grandfather's lap. In a dreamlike way I wondered how I had become the grandfather, and so quickly too. In some moments, life seems like nothing more than a dream.

Row, row, row your boat
Gently down the stream,
Merrily, merrily, merrily, merrily
Life is but a dream.

People say that things seem to happen as if in slow motion just prior to an accident. They say the experience is dreamlike. Or someone shows up in our life at just the right time and in just the right way and we say, "It's a dream come true."

Isn't a dream a sequence of images that evoke emotions and reactions that come and go? And is this not true of our waking life as well?

Life is but a dream.

When we walk down the street on a dark night, the wind speaks to us, the trees wave, and the squirrels wink. People come and go. The seasons change. One day we look in the mirror and see we have changed. When did that happen? We think that life is going to unfold one way and it goes and takes a different direction. This ends, that begins. We walk the maze of moments, but every turn we make begins a new beginning that never finds an ending. We go to the far horizon only to find a further horizon. It all seems so surprising.[1]

The dream changes from day to day. Sometimes it's a nightmare. Sometimes it makes no sense. Sometimes it makes us laugh. The changing landscape of our lives is nothing if not unpredictable.

In Mark's gospel, the story is told of how Jesus was talking to people on a village street when he was interrupted with the sad news that the child of the ruler of the synagogue had died. Jesus headed immediately for the girl's house, where he found family, friends and servants all crying their hearts out. Entering the house, Jesus asked them why there was all this tumult and weeping. After all, the child was not dead, she was only sleeping. As the people in the room laughed incredulously, Jesus took the father and mother to the child's bedside. Taking the girl by the hand, he told her to get up. And immediately she got up and walked.[2]

Was the girl dead or was she only sleeping? Was Jesus saying that being dead is like being asleep? Or being asleep is like being dead? What's the meaning of this story?

One way to interpret a Bible story is to take what the Bible says literally and believe that the way the Bible says it happened is how it really happened.

For example, we could believe that Jesus really did bring the man's daughter back to life. Literalism insists that the text means what it says and says what it means. For literalists, there are no shades of grey, no nuances of meaning, no metaphor or ambiguity. Everything is black or white. What you see is what you get.

When we take things literally, we confuse the words with what they stand for. We eat the menu because we believe it is the meal. We consume the words rather than searching for the truth behind them.

I like to think that the meaning of the story of Jesus raising the girl from the dead is more profound than the literal interpretation of Jesus waking up a little girl who everyone thought was dead. I take this story as a reminder or teaching that we human beings tend to go through life as if asleep, but the real purpose in life is to be awake. Jesus tells us we are here to be awake to the Holy Presence. The sleeping/dead girl represents the universal human condition of being asleep through our lives. I don't think this story is meant to be a demonstration of Jesus as Son of God with special powers. I believe this story is meant to teach us about waking up to life.

In 1980, the anthropologist Joan Halifax was studying the indigenous people of Ecuador, when she had an accident and sought out a shaman for healing. She writes about that experience in *Shaman: The Wounded Healer.*

A torrential rain thoroughly soaked me as I awkwardly climbed a slippery embankment on the way to the shaman's dwelling. I had broken my right arm that morning in an accident in a remote jungle in northern Ecuador. The healing ceremony that was to take place that night was not for my benefit but for those who had traveled from far distances in canoes and for the local sick. The dwelling was less like a domestic space and more like a hospital, with dozens of men, women, and children lying curled up on the split bamboo floor. The shaman began to enchant the spirits with his song, whistling, and with the rustling of the dry leaves that he played like a rattle. The candles were extinguished and a great silence fell upon all. I was curled up on a platform to the shaman's left, holding my throbbing arm, when I suddenly fell asleep. He traveled uninvited into my dreams. He came to me like a luminous body arriving in the ocean of my sleep. I knew he was there, although I had not been told that this was what he had to do in order to see my affliction and be given the cure.

Some fifteen hours later, in the early morning after the conclusion of the ceremony, I looked into the kind face of the shaman who had officiated at the ceremony, and the heat of recognition passed through me. I cannot describe, even to myself in a wordless way, the opening of compassion that seemed to happen between us. The spaciousness of that moment was ancient and familiar.[3]

Shamans and witch doctors, the recognized healers in ancient indigenous traditions, have always known what our medical schools are only now beginning to teach. It's people that are healed, not just illnesses. The shaman heals at the level of dreams and the unconscious because what is true in us when we are awake is true in us when we are asleep, and vice versa. The dreams we dream while sleeping are the other side of the dreams we live while we are awake. Two sides of the same coin. Awake or asleep, it's all a dream. Awake or asleep, life is a succession of images and experiences that give rise to feelings that come and go. Row, row, row your boat. Life is but a dream.

Ironically, waking up to life is to see it as a passing dream. When we open to life's magic and mystery, and to its impermanence and unpredictability, we behold a spiritual truth. Amidst the dreams and nightmares of life, waking up is seeing. I am in a dream, but I am not the dream. I am in a nightmare, but every nightmare passes. To wake up to life is to accept the dream as it is, as it comes to us.

St. Teresa of Avila said, "Let nothing upset you, let nothing frighten you; all things are passing; God does not change; patience sees the truth."[4] All the mystics tell us that to wake up to life is to see the passing dream, all the while knowing we are being held by God. God is always holding us.

But sometimes the details of the dream of life distract us and we forget we are being held safely.

The story of Bruno, a member of Lake Street Church, illustrates how we can wake up and remember we are being held by God. Bruno grew up in Eastern Europe, and in the early 1990s he came to the United States. When he first got here, he found a job in the building trades. Through a series of unfortunate circumstances, he found himself unemployed and ended up in the homeless shelter at Lake Street Church. While in the shelter, he became a member of the church, developing relationships and taking on responsibilities in the church community.

However, progress is rarely linear. As Bruno struggled to get back on his feet, things kept knocking him down. Then, just as he was turning a corner and things were getting better, he was diagnosed with colon cancer. Understandably, he felt as if life itself was conspiring against him.

To keep his cancer from spreading, the doctors insisted he undergo chemotherapy, which he agreed to. Halfway into the treatment, he was admitted to the emergency room with a pulmonary embolism. The pulmonary embolism sent him to the Intensive Care Unit.

Over the years spent as a homeless person, Bruno had adopted an oppositional attitude towards almost everyone who wanted to help him. This was a survival strategy. He did not trust anyone. The dream had become a long, lurid nightmare.

So when I visited him at the hospital, I expected to find an angry, despondent, depressed Bruno. But that's not what I found. I found instead a Bruno who exuded peace and equanimity.

I asked him what had changed for him. He said, "They told me the embolism could kill me. I thought, it's been bad, but I don't want to die. This experience changed me," he said. "I don't know how to explain it, but for the first time in a long time I feel safe. I believe the people in this hospital are on my side. I have let go. I've let go of thinking bad things about other people. Rather than suspecting everyone who comes in here, I think of everyone as a friend."

When we feel safe, even a nightmare cannot frighten us. When we feel safe, we see life as the dream it is. We know we are not the dream but the dreamer. We see the dream as something that happens to us, but we know we are not the dream. We awaken to the dream of life.

Back in the early 1980s, Lake Street Church considered becoming a "sanctuary church." Becoming a sanctuary church meant we would have welcomed illegal refugees from Central America who were seeking asylum and shelter. Becoming a sanctuary church was also an act of corporate civil disobedience. The government was threatening to prosecute sanctuary churches, which meant that our property could be confiscated and key church leaders thrown in jail. Some members of the congregation threatened to leave the church if we declared sanctuary.

It was a rough and tumultuous time. In the midst of this conflict, the erudite and dignified 80-year-old Josephine Grey walked up to me after worship service one Sunday and put her hand on my arm. "Deary," she said, "I am opposed to becoming a sanctuary church. But I want you to know, I've been through a lot in this church, I've seen a lot over the years, and I want you not to worry. We'll get through this and everything will be all right."

Her words were meant to be reassuring, but the conflict was so intense that I couldn't really believe them.

Now I know she wasn't saying that everything would turn out the way I wanted it to. She was saying that when everything turns out, it will be okay. Josephine was telling me that she was awake to the dream.

It turns out that homeless Bruno and high-society Josephine were both tapping into the same great wisdom. We are awake when we know the dream we're in isn't the final reality. We are awake when we know that life is nothing more than a passing show.

When we are awake, we know that no matter what happens we are always safe.

Awake to this truth, we are no longer asleep.

[1] *Anywhere Is* from *Paint the Sky with Stars* CD, Enya
[2] Mark 5:35–43
[3] Joan Halifax, *Shaman: The Wounded Healer* (Crossroad, 1983)
[4] Mirabai Starr, *The Interior Castle: St. Teresa of Avila* (Riverhead Books, 2003)

22

Every Tomb Is a Womb

$\cdots \:\:\mathcal{O}\!\mathcal{O}\!\mathcal{O}\!\mathcal{O}\:\:\cdots$

I remember a seminary professor who became upset to the point of shaking over a point of biblical theology. Puffing up and turning red in the face he lectured us, "Do not confuse the resurrection of Jesus Christ with the mere passing of the seasons. Many people confuse the Easter message with the coming of spring. But Easter is not about the rebirth of the earth, it is about the supernatural power of God."

By insisting that Easter was a supernatural, extraordinary, one of a kind miracle, my professor was differentiating between supernatural and natural power. Judging from his lecture, it seems unlikely that my professor was acquainted with the Goddess traditions of Northern Europe. The word Easter is derived from *Eostre*, the Nordic Goddess of spring. Celebrated as the Goddess of rebirth, *Eostre* was all about fertility. Coincidentally, people believed that rabbits and eggs were signs of her power.

It was the Council of Nicaea in 325 CE that established the date for Easter as the first Sunday after the full moon following the vernal equinox. Easter and spring have been close associates ever since. But what does the resurrection of Jesus have to do with the eternal rebirth of nature apart from the time of year?

The original intent of the Easter story was to highlight God's supernatural nature and reiterate that God had done something decisive and definitive for all of time. The resurrection of Jesus was interpreted as a once and for all supernatural feat. The dead Jesus came back to his body, got up and left his tomb. The evidence of the Resurrection was the empty tomb. The early Christian traditions said that the body of Jesus was raised from the dead and the empty tomb was proof.

My seminary professor's point was that Jesus' resurrection was a unique and unrepeatable occurrence. It did not have a deeper metaphorical meaning that linked it with a recurring seasonal event. It happened as read. It was amazing. It was a one-off.

Stories of great signs and wonders always point to invisible truths beyond the questionable facts. What is the essential meaning of resurrection if not dying to one way of life and rising to another? Resurrection is a truth of life itself, not something found only in the ancient story of Jesus. Resurrection happens in every moment throughout all of time. Everyone I know has a resurrection story to tell.

When we say goodbye to a person or place we love, a part of us dies. We are then reborn to another way of life. When we go through a divorce, lose a friendship, or fail to get the job we want, something in us dies while something else in us rises up.

How many times have we risen beyond where we were only to live where we are right now? We die hundreds, if not thousands, of deaths before our bodies breathe their last.

I do not know whether Jesus was literally raised from the dead. I did not see it or experience it. Maybe it happened the way the stories say, maybe it wasn't like that at all. But the story itself provides a clue about the essence of life.

Treating the Resurrection as an other-worldly and distant event implies that God showed up differently when Jesus was on earth.

Annie Dillard warns about limiting spiritual signs and wonders to a particular time.

> There were no formerly heroic times, and there was no formerly pure generation. There is no one here but us chickens, and so it has always been: a people busy and powerful, knowledgeable, ambivalent, important, fearful and self-aware; a people who scheme, promote, deceive and conquer; who pray for their loved ones, and long to flee misery and skip death. It is a weakening and discoloring idea that rustic people know God personally once upon a time...but that it is too late for us. In fact, the Absolute is available to everyone in every age. There never was a more holy age than ours, and never a less.
>
> There is no less holiness at this time...than there was the day the Red Sea parted...There is no whit less enlightenment under the tree by your street than there was under the Buddha's bodhi tree. ...In any instant the Sacred may wipe you with its finger...In any instant you may avail yourself of the power to love your enemies; to

accept failure, slander, or the grief of loss; or to endure torture.

Purity's time is always now…"Each and every day the Divine Voice issues from Sinai," says the Talmud. Of eternal fulfillment, Tillich said, "If it is not seen in the present, it cannot be seen at all."[1]

What we see depends on how we see. If spiritual signs and wonders are not obvious in the here and now, were they ever really? Have they always been around and we're just not noticing them? Or were they here before and now they're not? Is the Resurrection a fact of history or the eternal truth of human experience?

Easter tells us that the spirit of life is always alive and poised to bounce back. It can be oppressed, suppressed, depressed and suffocated, but it never dies. In a very profound sense, death is not only ahead of us, but also behind us. Most of the time what we fear is not death, but dying. It's the passing away of the familiar that frightens us so, not the arrival at the "other side."

Over the past millennia the story of Easter has been handed to us as freeze-dried dogma. But the real story is more like poetry in motion. There is, after all, much movement in resurrection. Rebirth is hardly static.

The gospels say that when Jesus died, it seemed like the end of the world. But it wasn't. Death is never the end of the world for anyone.

After Jesus had died, he got up again. He got up and he laughed. It wasn't the kind of laugh we laugh when we hear or see something funny. It was the kind of chuckling that comes over us when we realize our fears and worries have been pointless. Jesus got up laughing because death turned out to be one more joke. The end is the beginning. The tomb becomes a poignant metaphor for the womb. But we can only believe in the tomb as womb if we have experienced it for ourselves.

Speaking once again as a self-confessed heretic, I do not believe we are resurrected because Jesus was resurrected. Jesus was resurrected because resurrection is itself the power of life that is embedded in all of life. Transitions and transformations are woven into the very fabric of the universe. All of our lives are characterized by continuing deaths and resurrections. Winter becomes spring, spring becomes summer, and summer fades to fall.

In every moment there is transformation. Life is ongoing transitions from this to that, from that to this. And all of us have the fundamental power within us that enables us to rise up again, and again, and again. It is not that God has to reach down to pull us up because we can't do it ourselves. Rather, the Divine power whispers from within, "Rise up, rise up."

One bitterly cold day, when the whole earth was frozen and life seemed absent, Saint Francis turned toward an almond tree and called out, "Speak to me of God! Please, I need help. I am losing heart. Speak to me of God."

Gradually, branch by branch, the almond tree blossomed. The ice on the branches melted, beautiful flowers appeared and the whole tree became covered with blooms. The tree came alive naturally and completely.

This is how it happens. Like spring, resurrection awakens us to the eternal flow of life. God is not a supernatural power *over* us, but the natural power *within* us that allows us to rise up, again and again and again.

And still I rise, and still I rise, and still I rise.

Herein lies our true nature. Herein lies our resurrection and our spring.

---

1   Annie Dillard, *For the Time Being* (Knopf, 1999)

23

From Religious Tribalism to the City of God

I once heard Benedictine monk Brother David Steindl Rast sum up the history of the world's religions in two minutes. He said that most religions can trace their beginning to the mystical experiences of one charismatic person, such as Gautama Buddha, Moses, Jesus or Mohammed. In all cases, these inimitable teachers exuded such love and compassion that to be in their presence was to be standing on holy ground.

After their deaths, their followers memorialized them by building sacred shrines. They developed rituals that they followed in the hope that the original experience would be rekindled. They took the teachings and turned them into doctrines and moral codes.

The shrines, rituals, teachings and doctrines have been passed down from generation to generation for hundreds and even thousands of years, and present-day followers have to rely on tradition rather than first-hand experience.

Philosopher Huston Smith agrees that the world's main religions have an essential commonality. He says that they are like a pair of trousers: One at the top and plural at the bottom.[1]

On the mountaintop of mystical experience, Truth is one. Down in the valley of time and space, each religion develops its own unique teachings, rituals and ways of being in the world. In the valley of everyday life, Truth becomes the trouser legs and appears as truths. Life is plural, full of dichotomies, dualities, and pairs of opposites. In this valley, religion gets institutionalized.

When light is broken apart, or refracted, through a prism or water, white light appears as a rainbow spectrum of colour. If we think of Truth as light, each religion could represent a particular hue, but none is the full white Divine light itself. The light available in first-hand mystical experience is simply too grand and luminous to be mediated by one or more religious traditions. All religious perceptions imply, infer and point, but none captures all of the light. At best we see it indirectly.

As Emily Dickinson wrote:

Tell the truth but tell it slant
Success in Circuit lies
Too bright for our infirm Delight
The Truth's superb surprise
As Lightning to the Children eased
With explanations kind
The truth must dazzle gradually
Or every(one) be blind.

Each and every religious perspective leans in the direction of Truth. Religion is a trail, a path that points the way to Truth.

If you were to hold a beautifully cut jewel up to the light, you would see it gleaming in front of you. But if you were to turn the gem ever so slightly, you would see a different facet. If you were to turn it again, another aspect would be reflected. A faceted jewel has many aspects. What you see depends on where you stand in relation to it. What you see depends on how the light falls on it.

One jewel, one Truth. How I see, feel, and talk about it depends on the light available to me. Truth with a capital "T" does not change, nor is it relative. However, what we see is limited by the subjectivity of our perception, so we usually miss the whole Truth.

This is why it is important to cultivate interfaith relationships. When we share dialogue (*dia-logos* originally "the flow of meaning") with other traditions, an interesting thing happens. Seeing another facet of the jewel of Truth encourages us to explore our own tradition and assumptions more deeply.

A renowned Sufi author and teacher once gave a presentation on Sufism to a group of Christian ministers and priests. As the meeting was wrapping up, she said, "I have a question for all of you. I have never been able to understand this teaching that Jesus Christ was fully God and fully human and especially that he was the only one. Could someone please explain this to me?"

The room was utterly silent. One pastor recited a portion of the Nicene Creed, which sounded terribly hollow. Another said the question of Jesus' divinity is unanswerable and that it has to be taken on faith. More silence.

Finally one minister spoke up, saying, "Look, this is a tough question, and the truth is that all of us in this room are not in agreement. If we actually said what we really believed, blood would be shed."

Nervous giggles broke out. In shining her light on the jewel of Truth, that woman reminded those in the room that Christianity is not monolithic. Though limited, her light turned out to be more than we were accustomed to in our meetings. We left the room without answering the question.

Like many Protestant churches, The Lake Street Church of Evanston celebrates the first Sunday in October as World Communion Sunday. For more than a decade, we have celebrated this Sunday with an interfaith service comprising eight different religious traditions. We gather with Buddhists, Hindus, Sikhs, Jains, Jews and Muslims to celebrate not only our diversity but also our unity as human beings.

The very first year we held workshops on the Saturday before the interfaith service. As the various workshops began I sat in the hallway of our Church House. After a few moments I heard the sound of the om chant coming from the room where Hindus were leading. From across the hall came the sound of a Pali chant led by a Thai Buddhist monk. From upstairs came the sounds of a Sufi Dikhr, and then the Christian Taizé *Ubi Caritas*. Finally, the harmonium sent out its resonant tones as the Sikhs chanted out *Wahe Guru*, wonderful God. All of these disparate sounds seemed to wrap themselves around me. It was the strangest music I had ever heard. The sounds were not necessarily compatible musically, but they created a harmony that gave me goosebumps.

This new harmony requires us to understand that the purpose of our differences is to teach us how to make new music together.

The word *guru* means "dispeller of darkness" or "giver of light." One's own spiritual community can become like a guru. When Christians speak of the church being "the Body of Christ" the implication is the spiritual community is a giver of light. Buddhists speak of taking refuge in the Buddha, Dharma and the *sangha*, their spiritual community. For Muslims, the spiritual community is known as *Ummah*. In Judaism *kehilla* or *Klal Israel* expresses this truth.

In practically every religious and spiritual tradition there is the understanding that the spiritual community sheds more light on our lives than we can possibly see by ourselves.

Throughout this book I have been saying that Jesus' life and message proclaimed that spiritual community cannot be limited to proscribed sectarian boundaries. The late Brother Wayne Teasdale developed the term interspiritual.[2] He said that the dramatic shift in global human consciousness is preparing us to live in a universal civilization in which human beings recognize their spiritual interdependence. We can remain rooted in our own tradition, he said, without being stuck in it. Being rooted in a tradition is what keeps our feet on the ground. But we can also branch out. We branch out because more light is available than can be seen through the prism of our parochialisms. In this way we can cultivate a new and larger spiritual community; one that is rooted in our own tradition but not limited to it. We can move from a parochial understanding of religion to a universal understanding of interspirituality.

We are all a part of each other. In the Abrahamic traditions, there are admonitions to welcome the stranger. On his road to enlightenment the Buddha welcomed strangers and strange experiences. The Hindu sacred text, *The Upanishads*, says "Let a person never turn away a stranger from his house; that is the rule. Therefore a man should, by all means, acquire much food, for good people say to the stranger: 'There is enough food for you.'"[3]

The interspiritual community becomes a guru, a giver of light, as we learn to welcome the strangers of other communities into our own.

On a number of occasions, members of my congregation have engaged Buddhist, Muslim, Sikh and Hindu communities in dialogue. People have come together to share the things in their hearts.

At one gathering, a Hindu Swami spoke about Krishna consciousness while I spoke about Christ consciousness. Then people divided up into small mixed groups of Hindus and Christians. The conversation that ensued was enlightening for all. People held different perspectives and did not hesitate to express them. Everyone spoke and listened attentively. And all gathered with the deep conviction that there was something to be learned from those who were different.

People said that they had a glimpse of the jewel of Truth. The glimpse of Truth was not so much in the form of religious ideals, but in the blossoming of relationships. The jewel of Truth is revealed not in ideology, theology or beliefs but in the recognition that we are innately and inexorably connected.

The late Senator Paul Simon used to tell the story about a Special Olympics over which he presided. He told this story many times, and every time he told it he could scarcely finish it because it choked him up so.

In the story, disabled runners assemble at the starting line. The gun sounds and the racers sprint. About a third of the way through the race, one of the runners falls. The crowd gasps. With utter spontaneity, the rest of the runners stop in their tracks. They look in horror at the one who had fallen. Then, one by one, of their own accord, they turn around and slowly make their way back to help the fallen runner to his feet. They get him up and the race continues, with all of them running arm in arm to the finish line. They finish the race together. They recognize their interconnectedness. They are all winners.

We all fall. We all suffer. But we are called by the Spirit to move beyond our suffering and to join hands and help each other to the finish line. To move beyond religious tribalism to the interspiritual city of God requires an understanding, beyond dogma and belief, of what it means to be religious.

Mahatma Gandhi said, "You must watch my life. How I live, eat, sit, talk, and behave in general. The sum total of all those in me is my real religion."

In his poem *Manifesto: The Mad Farmer's Liberation Front*, Wendell Berry urges us to go beyond all forms of parochialism, not just religious tribalism. I'll let him speak the last words of this book.

So, friends, every day do something
That won't compute. Love the Lord.
Love the world. Work for nothing.
Take all that you have and be poor.
Love someone who does not deserve it.
Denounce the government and embrace
The flag. Hope to live in that free
Republic for which it stands.
Give your approval to all you cannot

Understand. Practice ignorance, for what man
Has not encountered what he has not destroyed.

Ask the questions that have no answers.
Invest in the millennium. Plant sequoias.
Say our main crop is the forest
That you did not plant,
That you will not live to harvest...[4]

So friends, do something that won't compute.

[1]   Huston Smith, *Why Religion Matters* (HarperSanFrancisco, 2001)
[2]   Wayne Teasdale, *The Mystic Heart* (The New World Library, 1999)
[3]   *The Upanishads: Translations from Sanskrit, introduction by Juan Mascaro* (Penguin Books, 1965)
[4]   Wendell Berry, *Collected Poems* (North Point Press, 1984)

Bibliography

••• ❦ •••

Bacevich, Andrew. *The New American Militarism*.
New York: Oxford University Press, 2005.

Backhouse, Halcyon, ed. *The Best of Meister Eckhart*.
New York: Crossroad, 1993.

Barasch, Marc. *Field Notes on the Compassionate Life*.
Emmaus, PA: Rodale, 2005.

Ben Shea, Noah. *Jacob the Baker*. New York: UAHC Press, 1990.

Berry, Wendell. *Collected Poems*.
San Francisco: North Point Press, 1984.

Borg, Marcus. *The Heart of Christianity*.
San Francisco: HarperSanFrancisco, 2003.

———. *Meeting Jesus Again for the First Time*.
San Francisco: HarperSanFrancisco, 1995.

Buechner, Frederick. *Secrets in the Dark*.
San Francisco: HarperSanFrancisco, 2006.

Chodron, Pema. *Start Where You Are*.
Boston: Shambhala, 1994.

———. *When Things Fall Apart*. Boston: Shambhala. 1997.

Coffin, William Sloane. *Credo*.
Louisville, KY: Westminster John Knox Press, 2004.

Crossan, John Dominic. *Jesus: A Revolutionary Biography*.
San Francisco: HarperSanFrancisco, 1994.

Cutler, Howard, and HH Dalai Lama. *The Art of Happiness*.
New York: Riverhead Books, 1998.

De Mello, Anthony. *The Heart of Enlightenment*.
New York: Image Books, 1991.

Dillard, Annie. *For the Time Being*. New York: Vintage, 1999.

Eck, Diana. *Encountering God: A Spiritual Journey from Bozeman to Banaras*. Boston: Beacon Press, 1993.

Feldman, Christina and Jack Kornfield. *Stories of the Spirit, Stories of the Heart*. New York: HarperCollins, 1991.

Flinders, Carol Lee. *Enduring Grace: Living Portraits of Seven Women Mystics*. San Francisco: HarperSanFrancisco, 1993.

Folwer, George. *Learning to Dance Inside: Getting to the Heart of Meditation*. Reading, MA: Addison Wesley, 1996.

Fosdick, Harry Emerson. *Successful Christian Living*. New York: Harper & Brothers, 1937.

Fox, Matthew. *Breakthrough: Meister Eckhart's Creation Spirituality in New Translation*. New York: Image Books, 1980.

Frankl, Viktor. *Recollections, an Autobiography*. Malibu, CA: Perseus Publishing, 2000.

Funk, Robert. *Honest to Jesus*. San Francisco: HarperSanFrancisco, 1996.

Hanh, Thich Nhat. *Peace Is Every Step*. Bantam Books, 1991.

Havel, Vaclav. *The Art of the Impossible, Translated from the Czech by Paul Wilson and others*. Fromm International, 1998.

Heschel, Abraham. *I Asked for Wonder*. New York: Crossroad, 1991.

Housden, Roger. *Seven Sins for a Life Worth Living*. New York: Harmony Books, 2005.

Kingsolver, Barbara. *Small Wonder.*
San Francisco: HarperSanFrancisco, 2002.

Lawrence, D. H. *The Complete Poems of D. H. Lawrence.*
Newton, KS: Wordsworth Editions Limited, 1994.

Nouwen, Henri. *Seeds of Hope.* New York: Image Books, 1997.

O'Neal, David. *Meister Eckhart, From Whom God Hid Nothing.*
Boston: Shambhala, 1996.

Prather, Hugh. *Spiritual Notes to Myself.* Berkeley, CA: Conari
Press, 1998.

Salzberg, Sharon. *Faith: Trusting Your Own Deeper Experience.*
New York: Riverhead Books, 2002.

Schweitzer, Albert. *The Spiritual Life – Selected Writings of Albert
Schweitzer.* Hopewell, NJ: Ecco, 1947.

Shah, Idries. *Nasrudin. Volumes 1, 2, 3.*
New York: E. P. Dutton and Co., 1973.

Singh, Rajinder. *The Silken Thread of the Divine.*
Naperville, IL: S. K. Publications, 2005.

———. *Empowering the Soul through Meditation.*
New York: Element Books, 2003.

Smith, Huston. *Why Religion Matters.*
San Francisco: HarperSanFrancisco, 2001.

Starr, Mirabai. The *Interior Castle, St. Teresa of Avila.*
Tampa, FL: River Books, 2004.

Teasdale, Wayne. *The Mystic Heart.*
Novato, CA: New World Library, 1999.

Tillich, Paul. *Systematic Theology.* Volumes 1-3.
Chicago: University of Chicago Press, 1967.

Ury, William. *The Third Side.* New York: Penguin Books, 2000.

Washington, James M., ed. *A Testament of Hope: The Essential Writings and Speeches of Martin Luther King.*
San Francisco: HarperSanFrancisco, 1986.

Wink, Walter. *The Powers That Be.* New York: Galilee, 1998.